NASHVILLE

SUSANNA HENIGHAN POTTER

Contents

NASHVILLE 9

Planning Your Time. 10
When To Go 11

Orientation. 11
City Center......................... 11
East Nashville 11
North Nashville 13
West Nashville..................... 13
South Nashville 14

Sights. 15

Broadway And The District. 15
(Country Music Hall Of Fame 15
The Ryman Auditorium 16
Shelby Street Pedestrian Bridge 16
Fort Nashborough.................. 17
Tennessee Sports Hall Of Fame 17
Customs House 17
Hume Fogg....................... 17
The Frist Center For The Visual Arts .. 17

Downtown. 17
Tennessee State Capitol 20
Tennessee State Museum 21
(Civil Rights Room At The Nashville
    Public Library 21
The Arcade....................... 22
Downtown Presbyterian Church...... 22

Music Row. 23
Rca Studio B 23
The Upper Room................... 23

Midtown. 23
(The Parthenon.................. 23
Belmont Mansion 26
Vanderbilt University 27
Belmont University................. 28

West End. 28
Belle Meade Plantation 28
(Cheekwood...................... 29

South Nashville 30
Fort Negley 30
City Cemetery 31
Adventure Science Center.......... 31
Tennessee Central Railway Museum .. 33
Nashville Zoo At Grassmere 33
Travellers Rest Plantation
    And Museum................... 33
Tennessee Agricultural Museum...... 34

Jefferson Street 34
Bicentennial Mall.................. 34
Fisk University..................... 35
Meharry Medical College........... 37
Hadley Park 37
Tennessee State University......... 38

Music Valley. 38
The Grand Ole Opry 39

East Of Nashville. 39
(The Hermitage.................. 39

Tours. 42
Nash Trash Tours 42
Gray Line Tours................... 42
General Jackson Showboat.......... 42
Tennessee Central Railway 42
Nashville Black Heritage Tours....... 42

Entertainment 43

Live Music And Clubs. 43
(The Grand Ole Opry 43
Ernest Tubb Midnite Jamboree....... 45
The Gibson Showcase.............. 45
The Ryman Auditorium 45
Country Music Hall Of Fame 45
(The Bluebird Cafe 45
Clubs........................... 46

Concert Series 49

Bars. 49
The District 49
Printer's Alley 50

Midtown 50
East Nashville 50
12 South 51
Gay And Lesbian Nightlife 51
Comedy 51
The Arts 51
Theater 51
Children's Theater 52
Music 53
Opera 53
Ballet 53
Dinner Theater 53
Cinemas 53
Events 54
February 54
April 54
May 55
June 55
July 55
August 55
September 56
October 56
November 56
December 56
Shopping 56
Music 56
Western Wear 57
Clothing 57
Art 58
Home Decor 58
Books 58
Antiques 59
Malls 59
Outlet Malls 59
Flea MarkeTs .59
Sports And Recreation 60
Parks 60
Centennial Park 60
Radnor Lake State Natural Area 60
Edwin And Percy Warner Parks 60
J. Percy Priest Lake 60
Golf 61

Biking 61
Bike Shops 62
Resources 62
Tennis 62
Swimming 62
Gyms 63
Spectator Sports 63
Football 63
Racing 63
Baseball 63
Soccer 63
Ice Hockey 64
College Sports 64
Accommodations 64
Broadway And The District 64
Downtown 65
Midtown 66
East Nashville 67
Music Valley 68
Airport 69
South Of Nashville 69
Food 70
Diners And Coffee Shops 70
Southern Specialties 72
Barbecue 74
Steakhouses 75
Contemporary 75
Ethnic Cuisine 76
Markets 78
Information And Services . . .79
Information .79
Visitors Centers 79
Maps 79
Media 79

Services............................80
  Internet..........................80
  Postal Service 80
  Emergency Services................80
  Libraries.........................80

Getting There And Around ..80
  Getting There 80
    By Air 80
    By Car.......................... 81
    By Bus.......................... 81

  Getting Around.................... 81
    Driving 81
    Public Transportation...........82
    Taxis 82

OUTSIDE NASHVILLE............83
Planning Your Time...............83

Franklin 86
Sights...........................86
  Mclemore House..................86
  Carnton Plantation..............86
  Fort Granger 87
  The Carter House 89

Entertainment 90
  Theater.........................90
  Live Music 90

Shopping.........................90
  Antiques........................90
  Downtown........................90
  The Factory 91
  Cool Springs Galleria 91

Accommodations.................. 91

Food.............................92

Information 93

Walking Horse Country......93
Bell Buckle 93
  Sights 94
  Events..........................94
  Shopping 94
  Accommodations 94
  Food 94
  Information 95

Wartrace.........................95
  Accommodations 95
  Food 97
  Information 97

Normandy.........................97
  George Dickel Distillery 97
  Accommodations 98
  Food 99

Lynchburg........................99
  Jack Daniel's Distillery........99
  Other Sights.................... 101
  Accommodations 101
  Food 101

The Natchez Trace 102

Leiper's Fork 102
  Shopping 102
  Entertainment 102
  Hiking 103
  Accommodations 103
  Food 103
  Information 104

Spring Hill......................104
  Rippavilla 105
  Tennessee Museum Of
    Early Farm Life 107
  General Motors Plant 109
  Accommodations 109

Columbia 109
  Ancestral Home Of
    James Knox Polk 109
  Events......................... 110

Accommodations 111
Food 111
Information 111

Land Between The Lakes 112

Sights 112
Great Western Iron Furnace 112
◖ The Homeplace 112
Elk And Bison Prairie 113

Recreation 113
Trails 114
Fishing And Boating 114
Hunting 114

Camping 114
Piney Campground 114
Energy Lake 115
Backcountry Camping 115

Practicalities .115

Fort Donelson National
Battlefield 115

Dover 115
Accommodations 115
Food 117
Information 117

NASHVILLE

NASHVILLE

Nashville is the home of country music. This city of 600,000 on the banks of the Cumberland River is where tomorrow's hits are made and where you can hear them performed on the stage of the longest-running live radio variety show, the Grand Ole Opry.

There is a twang in the air all around the city—in the honky-tonks along lower Broadway, on the streets of downtown Nashville, and in Music Valley, modern home of the Opry. During the annual Country Music Association Festival in June, the whole city is alive with the foot-tapping rhythm of country music.

Nashville is also the city where performers and songwriters come to make it in the music business. Listening rooms and nightclubs all over the city are the beneficiaries of this abundance of hopeful talent. There is no excuse to stay home after night falls.

It is wrong to think that country music is all there is to Nashville. After the Civil War and Reconstruction, Nashville became known as the Athens of the South because it was a center for education and the arts. Still today, Nashville offers visitors much more than a night at the Opry. Excellent art museums include the Frist Center for Visual Arts and the Cheekwood. The Nashville Symphony Orchestra plays in the elegant and acclaimed Schermerhorn Center downtown.

Come to watch the Tennessee Titans play football, or to play golf at one of the award-winning courses nearby. Admire the Parthenon in Centennial Park, or drive to the southern

PHOTO COURTESY THE TENNESSEE DEPARTMENT OF TOURIST DEVELOPMENT

HIGHLIGHTS

◖ Country Music Hall of Fame: Pay homage to the kings and queens of country music while you trace its evolution from old-time Appalachian mountain music to today's mega-hits (page 15).

◖ Civil Rights Room at the Nashville Public Library: The public library houses the best exhibit about the historic Nashville sit-ins of 1960 (page 21).

◖ The Parthenon: First built in 1897 to mark the 100th anniversary of the state of Tennessee, this life-sized replica of the Greek Parthenon is as beautiful as it is unusual (page 23).

◖ Cheekwood: Art and nature are perfectly balanced in this exceptional museum and botanic garden built on an estate financed by Maxwell House coffee (page 29).

◖ The Hermitage: The home of U.S. president Andrew Jackson is much more than a beautiful home; it is a museum of the 19th-century way of life (page 39).

◖ The Grand Ole Opry: The live radio variety show that's been on the air for more than 80 years is still the best place to be entertained in Music City (page 43).

◖ The Bluebird Cafe: The quintessential Nashville listening room, the Bluebird hosts intimate music sessions every night of the week (page 45).

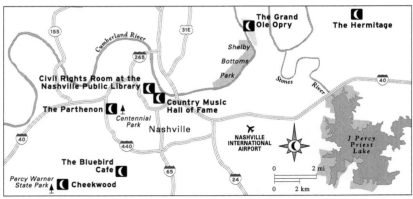

LOOK FOR ◖ TO FIND RECOMMENDED SIGHTS, ACTIVITIES, DINING, AND LODGING.

outskirts of the city for a hike at Radnor Lake State Natural Area.

Downtown is dominated by tall office towers and imposing government buildings, including the state Capitol. Meat-and-three restaurants serve irresistible Southern-style meals, while eateries along Nolensville Pike reflect the ethnic diversity of the city.

Nashville is a city that strikes many notes, but sings in perfect harmony.

PLANNING YOUR TIME

Nashville is a popular destination for weekend getaways. Over two days you can see a few of the city's attractions and catch a show at the Grand Ole Opry. Musical pilgrims and history enthusiasts should plan to spend more time in Music City. Even the most disciplined explorers will find themselves happily occupied if they choose to stay a full week.

Downtown is a good home base for many

visitors. Hotels here are within walking distance of many attractions, restaurants, and nightclubs. They are also the most expensive accommodations in the city. Visitors who are primarily interested in seeing a show at the Grand Ole Opry or shopping at Opry Mills should shack up in Music Valley, where you will find a smorgasbord of affordable hotel rooms.

Visitors with a car can also look for accommodation outside of the city center. There are affordable hotels in midtown, and charming bed-and-breakfasts in Hillsboro and East Nashville. All these neighborhoods are nicely off the tourist track. The city's lone hostel is in midtown and is a good choice for budget travelers.

When to Go

Summer is the most popular time to visit Nashville. The CMA Music Festival in June draws thousands to the city. Temperatures in August top out around 90 degrees, although it can feel much hotter.

Spring and fall enjoy mild temperatures, and are the best time to visit Nashville. You will avoid the largest crowds but still sample all that the city has to offer. In spring you will enjoy sights of tulips, dogwoods, and magnolias in bloom. Beginning in mid-October, foliage around the city starts to turn blazing red, brown, and yellow.

In winter, temperatures range from 30 to 50 degrees. During November and December, holiday concerts and decorations liven up the city. Many attractions cut back hours during winter, and some outdoor attractions are closed altogether.

ORIENTATION

For a city of its size, Nashville takes up a lot of space. In fact, Nashville has the second-largest footprint of any major American city. But don't picture a scene of concrete: Nashville is a leafy, suburban city. Outside downtown is a patchwork of traffic lights, strip malls, and tree-lined residential neighborhoods, several of which are incorporated towns with their own elected officials, city halls, and police.

Nashville's attractions are spread out among the city's various neighborhoods. Learn the locations and identities of a few parts of town, and you are well on your way to understanding Music City.

City Center

Nashville straddles the Cumberland River, a waterway that meanders a particularly uneven course in this part of Tennessee. Downtown Nashville sits on the west bank of the river, climbing a gradual incline from Broadway to the Tennessee State Capitol. It is defined by landmarks including the BellSouth tower, the tallest building in Tennessee, better known by many as the Batman building for the two tall antennae that spring from the top.

Downtown is divided into two general areas: **Broadway and the District** is the entertainment area, and where you will find major attractions like the Country Music Hall of Fame, the Ryman Auditorium, and Printer's Alley, a hotbed of clubs and bars. **Downtown** refers to the more traditional city zone, where you'll find office buildings, the Tennessee State Museum, and city parks.

It is a good plan to walk around central Nashville since traffic and parking are about as difficult here as in any city of this size. But do remember that Nashville is built on a hill. Walking between Broadway and the state Capitol is perfectly doable, but on a hot summer day, or with small children in tow, you may think otherwise.

East Nashville

Shelby Street Pedestrian Bridge spans the Cumberland at McGavock Street and takes you straight to the heart of East Nashville. Now dominated by humongous LP Field, home of the Tennessee Titans, the eastern reaches of Nashville are also home to some of the most charming residential neighborhoods. **Edgefield,** Nashville's oldest suburb, was a separate city when it first sprang up in the 19th century. Many of its most elegant homes were destroyed in the great East Nashville fire of 1916, but it still boasts a lovely mix of

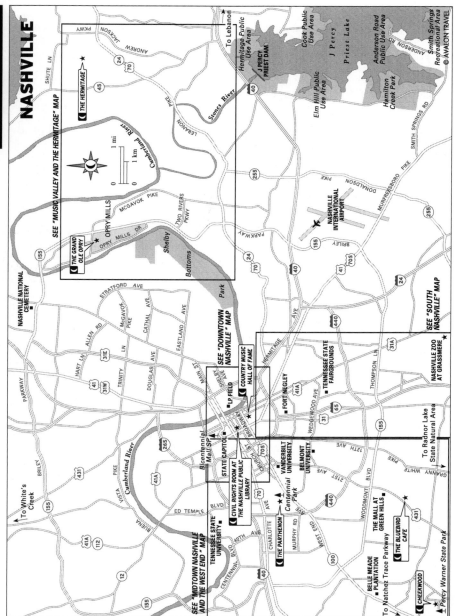

© SUSANNA HENIGHAN POTTER

Downtown Nashville sits on the west bank of the Cumberland River.

Victorian, Princess Anne, and Colonial Revival homes. Farther east is **Lockeland Springs.**

While there are no blockbuster attractions in East Nashville, visitors should consider the growing number of bed-and-breakfast accommodations here. The neighborhoods are close to downtown, but also boast their own unique nightlife, restaurants, and character.

North Nashville

North of the state Capitol and Bicentennial Mall is **Germantown,** a quaint, compact neighborhood now awash with galleries, restaurants, and studios, once the home of European immigrants. Heading west from Germantown, **Jefferson Street** takes you past several of Nashville's African-American landmarks, including Fisk University and Meharry Medical College.

A neighborhood created entirely for the tourist trade, **Music Valley** is the zone of hotels, restaurants, and retail that has popped up around the Opryland Hotel and the Grand Ole Opry House. Located inside a narrow loop of the Cumberland River, Music Valley lies northeast of downtown Nashville. It is convenient to the airport along the Briley Parkway.

If Music Valley is actually a valley, you wouldn't know it. The strip of hotels, restaurants, souvenir shops, and malls is just about as far removed from the natural environment as you can get. The Grand Ole Opry is the best thing that Music Valley has going for it. Opryland Hotel is an attraction in its own right, however, and Opry Mills is a discount shopper's paradise. Music Valley is also home to a wide variety of hotel accommodations, including some budget-friendly choices.

West Nashville

Perhaps the most famous neighborhood in all of Nashville, **Music Row** is where country music deals are done. The tree-lined streets of 16th and 17th Avenues, a few blocks southwest of downtown, shade dozens of different recording studios, record labels, and producers.

Lying just west of downtown, **Elliston Place** is a block of nightclubs, restaurants, and two famous Nashville eateries: Elliston Place Soda Shop and Rotier's.

The neighborhood is surrounded by medical complexes, and is a few blocks from the city's only downtown hostel. Centennial Park, Nashville's best urban park, is a few blocks farther west.

The youthful energy of nearby Vanderbilt University and Belmont College keep **Hillsboro Village** one of the most consistently hip neighborhoods in Nashville. Located on both sides of 21st Avenue, Hillsboro and the related neighborhood of Belmont are about as far away from the Grand Ole Opry as you can get in Nashville.

Hillsboro is home to one of Nashville's finest used book stores, stylish and pricey boutiques, and notable restaurants, including the upscale Sunset Grill, the down-home Pancake Pantry, and Fido, a coffeehouse for all seasons. Hillsboro is also where you will find the alternative movie house the Belcourt, which screens independent and arts movies every day of the week.

South of Hillsboro is **Green Hills,** whose primary attraction is a shopping mall. Together, Hillsboro, Elliston Place, and Green Hills are Nashville's **Midtown.**

Sylvan Park is an old suburb of the city, located between Charlotte Avenue and Murphy Road, just west of the city center. Noted for neat homes and state-named roads, the neighborhood is quiet and residential.

Along Charlotte Avenue, facing Sylvan Park, you will find antiques and thrift stores, the Darkhorse Theater, and Rhino Books, specializing in used and rare books. Farther out along Charlotte is the Goodwill Superstore, a dream come true for thrift store aficionados, and a burgeoning number of ethnic eateries.

West End refers to the neighborhoods along West End Avenue. It includes Belle Meade, an incorporated city and one of the wealthiest in the whole state. Head in this direction to find good restaurants, the Belle Meade Plantation, and Cheekwood.

South Nashville

South of the city center are several distinct neighborhoods. **8th Avenue South,** close to downtown, is the antiques district. Restaurants like Arnold's Country Kitchen and clubs including the Douglas Corner Cafe draw people to this neighborhood.

Follow 12th Avenue as it heads south from downtown to find **the Gulch.** Rising from what was once a railroad wasteland, the Gulch is now the city's hot spot for high-rise housing and urban condos.

A few miles farther south along 12th Avenue is **12 South,** another of Nashville's most newly gentrified neighborhoods. An influx of young professional property owners has given rise to new restaurants, boutiques, and coffee shops.

There is not much greenery left in **Green Hills,** a retail hot spot south of Hillsboro Village. If you can stand the traffic jam, follow 21st Avenue south to find upscale Green Hills Mall and the venerable Bluebird Cafe, tucked away in a strip mall a few blocks farther south.

Sights

BROADWAY AND THE DISTRICT

This is the entertainment and retail hub of Nashville. Walk along lower Broadway, as the blocks from 5th Avenue to the river are called, and you will pass a dozen different bars, restaurants, and shops catering to visitors. The District, located along 2nd Avenue near where it crosses Broadway, is a neighborhood where old warehouses have been converted to nightclubs, shops, office space, and loft condominiums.

◖ Country Music Hall of Fame

The distinctive design of the Country Music Hall of Fame and Museum (222 5th Ave. S., 615/416-2001, www.countrymusichalloffame.com, daily 9 A.M.–5 P.M., $15.95–19.95) is the first thing you will notice about this monument to country music. Vertical windows at the front and back of the building resemble

piano keys; the sweeping arch on the right side of the building portrays a 1950s Cadillac fin; and from above, the building resembles a bass clef. The Hall of Fame was first established in 1967, and its first inductees were Jimmie Rodgers, Hank Williams, and Fred Rose. The original Hall was located on Music Row, but in 2002 it moved to this brand-new signature building two blocks off Broadway in downtown Nashville.

Country music fans are drawn by the carload to the Hall of Fame, where they can pay homage to country's greatest stars, as well as the lesser-known men and women who influenced the music. The hall's slogan is "Honor Thy Music."

The museum is arranged chronologically, beginning with country's roots in the Scotch-Irish ballads sung by the southern mountains' first settlers, and ending with displays on some of the genre's hottest stars of today. In between,

Guitars and fringed jackets are some of the things on display at the Country Music Hall of Fame.

exhibits detail themes including the rise of bluegrass, honky tonk, and the world-famous Nashville Sound, which introduced country music to the world.

There are a half-dozen private listening booths where you can hear studio-quality recordings of seminal performances, as well as a special display of a few of the genre's most famous instruments. Here you can see Bill Monroe's mandolin, Maybelle Carter's Gibson, and Johnny Cash's Martin D-355.

If you are truly interested in learning something about country music while you're here, splurge on the $5 audio guide, which adds depth to the exhibits and helps to drown out distractions caused by your fellow museumgoers.

The Hall of Fame itself is set in a rotunda. Brass plaques honor the 100 inductees, and around the room are the words "Will the Circle Be Unbroken," from the hymn made famous by the Carter Family.

The Ryman Auditorium

Thanks to an $8.5 million renovation in the 1990s, the historic Ryman Auditorium (116 5th Ave. N., 615/889-3060, www.ryman.com, daily 9 A.M.–4 P.M., $12.50–16.25) remains one of the best places in the United States—let alone Nashville—to hear live music. Built in 1892 by Captain Thomas Ryman, the Union Gospel Tabernacle, as the Ryman was then called, was designed as a venue for the charismatic preaching of Rev. Samuel P. Jones, to whom Ryman owed his own conversion to Christianity.

Managed by keen businesswoman Lula C. Naff during the first half of the 20th century, the Ryman began to showcase music and performances. In 1943, Naff agreed for the Ryman to host a popular barn dance called the Grand Ole Opry. The legacy of this partnership gave the Ryman its place in history as the so-called Mother Church of Country Music.

The Opry remained at the Ryman for the next 31 years. After the Opry left in 1974, the Ryman fell into disrepair and was virtually condemned when Gaylord Entertainment, the same company that owns the Opry, decided to invest in the grand old tabernacle. Today, it is a

popular concert venue, booking rock, country, and classical acts, and performers still marvel at the fabulous acoustics of the hall.

Seeing a show at the Ryman is by far the best way to experience this historic venue, but if you can't do that, pay the $12.50 admission to see a short video and explore the auditorium on your own. You can sit a few minutes on the old wooden pews and even climb on stage to be photographed in front of the classic Opry backdrop. A guided tour that takes you backstage costs $16.25.

Shelby Street Pedestrian Bridge

Built in 1909, the Sparkman Street Bridge was slated for demolition in the 1998 after inspectors called its condition "poor." But citing the success of the Walnut Street Bridge in revitalizing downtown Chattanooga, Tennessee, advocates succeeded in saving the bridge. The Shelby Street Bridge reotpened in 2003 as a pedestrian and bike bridge.

The Shelby Street Bridge connects East

The Ryman Auditorium is also called the Mother Church of Country Music.

© SUSANNA HENIGHAN POTTER

Nashville neighborhoods with downtown. It is also convenient on Titan game days since the eastern terminus is a few hundred yards from LP Field. Perhaps most significant for visitors, however, is the fact that the views of the downtown cityscape are excellent from here.

Fort Nashborough

Fort Nashborough (170 1st Ave., 615/862-8400, Mon.–Sat. 10 A.M.–5:30 P.M., Sun. 1–5 P.M., free) is a one-quarter-sized replica of the fort erected by James Robertson and John Donelson when they first settled what was then called French Lick on Christmas Day 1779. Visitors here will get the feeling that this site has seen better days. While the replica fort is open, it is mostly left unattended and there is little to see or learn here. The interiors of the five cabins have been gated with iron bars, seemingly to prevent neighborhood vagrants from settling in. The site is mostly fascinating simply because it looks so out of place among Nashville's skyscrapers and the Tennessee Titans' stadium nearby. It has a nice view of the river too.

Tennessee Sports Hall of Fame

Sports fans will enjoy the Tennessee Sports Hall of Fame (Nashville Arena, 615/242-4750, www.tshf.net, Mon.–Sat. 10 A.M.–5 P.M., $3). Located in a state-of-the-art 7,500-square-foot exhibit space, the hall chronicles the history of sports in Tennessee from the 1800s to today's heroes.

Customs House

Located at 701 Broadway, the old Nashville Customs House is a historic landmark and architectural beauty. Construction on the Customs House began in 1875 and President Rutherford B. Hayes visited Nashville to lay the cornerstone in 1877. The building is an impressive example of the Victorian Gothic style. It was designed by Treasury architect William Appleton Potter and was completed in 1916. Although it is called a customs house, the building served as the center of federal government operations in the city:

Federal government offices, courts, and treasury offices were housed in the building. For many years it held the city's U.S. Post Office.

Ownership transferred from the federal to the city government in 1979 and the building was later leased for redevelopment. It currently houses federal bankruptcy court and other offices.

Hume Fogg

Located across Broadway from the Customs House is Hume Fogg Magnet School. It sits on land formerly occupied by Hume School, Nashville's first public school. The four-story stone-clad 1912 building was designed by William Ittner of St. Louis in the Norman Gothic style with Tudor Gothic details. Today, it is a public magnet school with a reputation for high academic standards.

The Frist Center for the Visual Arts

Nashville's foremost visual art space is the Frist Center for the Visual Arts (919 Broadway, 615/744-3247, www.fristcenter.org, Mon.–Sat. 10 A.M.–5:30 P.M., Thurs. and Fri. until 9 P.M., Sun. 1–5 P.M., adults $8.50, seniors and military $7.50, students $6.50). The Frist is located in a stately building that once housed the 1930s downtown post office. High ceilings, art deco finishes, and unique hardwood tiles distinguish the museum.

With no permanent collection of its own, the Frist puts on about 12 different major visiting exhibitions annually. At any given time, you will see between three and four different exhibits. ArtQuest, a permanent part of the Frist, is an excellent hands-on arts activity room for children and their parents.

DOWNTOWN

The greater part of downtown is dominated by large office buildings and federal, state, and city government structures. From Commerce Street northward to the state Capitol, you will find historic churches, museums, and hordes of office workers.

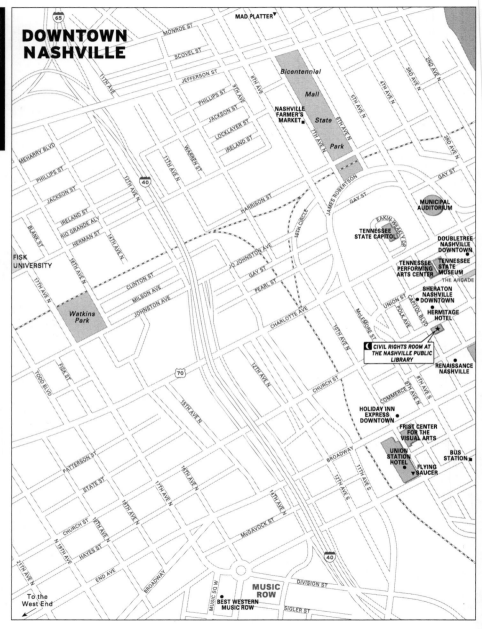

DOWNTOWN NASHVILLE

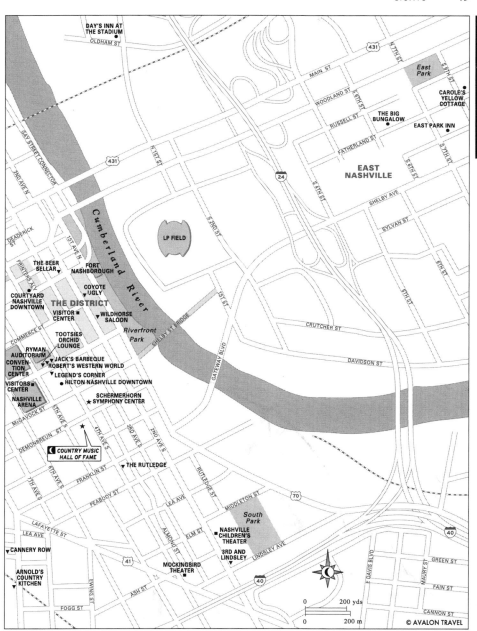

DAY'S INN AT THE STADIUM

OLDHAM ST

MAIN ST

431

N 7TH ST

S 8TH ST

East Park

WOODLAND ST

S 5TH ST

CAROLE'S YELLOW COTTAGE

RUSSELL ST

THE BIG BUNGALOW

EAST PARK INN

FATHERLAND ST

S 5TH ST

GAY STREET CONNECTOR

2ND AVE N

431

N 1ST ST

24

S 4TH ST

EAST NASHVILLE

S 6TH ST

SHELBY AVE

DEADERICK ST

Cumberland River

1ST AVE N

SYLVAN ST

LP FIELD

S 2ND ST

6TH ST

PRINTERS ALY

THE BEER SELLAR

FORT NASHBOROUGH

COYOTE UGLY

5TH ST

COURTYARD NASHVILLE DOWNTOWN

THE DISTRICT

VISITOR CENTER

WILDHORSE SALOON

1ST ST

SHELBY ST BRIDGE

CRUTCHER ST

COMMERCE ST

Riverfront Park

TOOTSIES ORCHID LOUNGE

GATEWAY BLVD

RYMAN AUDITORIUM

CONVENTION CENTER

JACK'S BARBEQUE

ROBERT'S WESTERN WORLD

DAVIDSON ST

VISITORS CENTER

LEGEND'S CORNER

HILTON NASHVILLE DOWNTOWN

NASHVILLE ARENA

SCHERMERHORN SYMPHONY CENTER

McGAVOCK ST

5TH AVE S

4TH AVE S

3RD AVE S

2ND AVE S

DEMONBREUN ST S

COUNTRY MUSIC HALL OF FAME

FRANKLIN ST

RUTLEDGE ST

6TH AVE S

THE RUTLEDGE

7TH AVE S

PEABODY ST

LEA AVE

MIDDLETON ST

70

LAFAYETTE ST

South Park

40

LEA AVE

ALMOND ST

ELM ST

NASHVILLE CHILDREN'S THEATER

LINDSLEY AVE

CANNERY ROW

41

3RD AND LINDSLEY

GREEN ST

ARNOLD'S COUNTRY KITCHEN

EWING ST

MOCKINGBIRD THEATER

ASH ST

40

F DAVIS BLVD

MAURY ST

FAIN ST

FOGG ST

CANNON ST

0   200 yds

0   200 m

© AVALON TRAVEL

© SUSANNA HENIGHAN POTTER

The Tennessee Senate chambers are inside the State Capitol.

Tennessee State Capitol

Set on the top of a hill and built with the formality and grace of classic Greek architecture, the capitol building of Tennessee strikes a commanding pose overlooking downtown Nashville. Construction of the Capitol began in 1845, two years after the state legislature finally agreed that Nashville would be the permanent capital city. Even with the unpaid labor of convicts and slaves, it took 14 years to finish the building.

The Capitol is built of limestone, much of it from a quarry located near present-day Charlotte and 13th Avenues. In the 1950s, extensive renovations were carried out and some of the original limestone was replaced. The interior marble came from Rogersville and Knoxville, and the gasoliers were ordered from Philadelphia. The Capitol was designed by architect William Strickland, who considered it his crowning achievement and is buried in a courtyard on the north end of the Capitol.

Visitors are welcome at the Capitol. Ask at the information desk for a printed guide that identifies each of the rooms and many of the portraits and sculptures both inside and outside of the building. If the legislature is not in session, you can go inside both the House and Senate chambers, which look much as they did back in the 19th century. In the 2nd-floor lobby, you can see two bronze reliefs depicting the 19th and 14th amendments to the United States Constitution, both of which were ratified by the State of Tennessee in votes held at the Capitol.

Guided tours of the Capitol depart hourly Monday–Friday 9 A.M.–3 P.M. Ask at the information desk inside for more information.

Other important State buildings surround the Capitol. The **Library and Archives** sits directly west of the Capitol, and next to the **Tennessee Supreme Court.** The **Tennessee War Memorial** is a stone plaza on the south side of the Capitol, and a nice place to people-watch. A number of State office buildings are nearby, and State employees can be seen walking to and fro, especially at lunchtime.

Tennessee State Museum

If you are used to the flashy multimedia exhibits found in many of today's top museums, the Tennessee State Museum (5th Ave., 615/741-2692, www.tnmuseum.org, Tues.–Sat. 10 A.M.–5 P.M., Sun. 1–5 P.M., free) will seem like a musty throwback to the past. The displays are largely straightforward combinations of text and images, and they require visitors to read and examine on their own. There are but a few video presentations. But for patrons with enough patience to give the displays their due, the museum offers an excellent overview of Tennessee history from the Native Americans to the New South era of the 1880s.

Exhibits detail the state's political development, the Revolutionary and Civil Wars, and profile famous Tennesseans including Andrew Jackson and Davy Crocket. They also cast a spotlight on the lifestyles and diversions of Tennesseans of various eras, from the early frontiersmen and -women to a free African-American family before emancipation. Special artifacts include the top hat worn by Andrew Jackson at his presidential inauguration, a musket that belonged to Daniel Boone, and the jaw bone of a mastodon.

The **Tennessee Military Museum** (Legislative Plaza, 615/741-2692, Tues.–Sat. 10 A.M.–5 P.M., free) is associated with the Tennessee State Museum and highlights America's overseas conflicts, beginning with the Spanish-American War in 1989 and ending with World War II. The exhibits examine the beginnings of the wars, major battles, and the outcomes. There is a special exhibit about Alvin C. York, the Tennessee native and World War I hero. The military museum is located in the War Memorial Building on the south side of the Capitol.

◖ Civil Rights Room at the Nashville Public Library

The Nashville Public Library (615 Church St., 615/862-5800, Mon.–Thurs. 9 A.M.–8 P.M., Fri. 9 A.M.–6 P.M., Sat. 9 A.M.–5 P.M., Sun. 2–5 P.M., free) houses the city's best exhibit on the movement for civil rights that took place in Nashville in the 1950s and '60s. Nashville was the first Southern city to desegregate public services, and it did so relatively peacefully, setting an example for activists throughout the south.

The story of the courageous men and women who made this change happen is told through photographs, videos, and displays in the Civil Rights Room at the public library. The library is a fitting location for the exhibit, since the block below on Church Street was the epicenter of the Nashville sit-ins during 1960.

Inside the room, large-format photographs show school desegregation, sit-ins, and a silent march to the courthouse. A circular table at the center of the room is symbolic of the lunch counters where young students from Fisk, Meharry, American Baptist, and Tennessee A&I sat silently and peacefully at sit-ins. The table is engraved with the ten rules of conduct set out for sit-in participants, including rules to be polite and courteous at all times, regardless of how you are treated. A timeline of the national and Nashville civil rights movements is presented above the table.

Inside a glass-enclosed viewing room you can choose from six different documentary videos, including an hour-long 1960 NBC news documentary about the Nashville sit-ins. Many of the videos are 30 minutes or longer, so plan on spending several hours here if you are keenly interested in the topics.

The centerpiece of the Civil Rights Room is a glass inscription by Martin Luther King, who visited the city in 1960 and said, during a speech at Fisk University: "I came to Nashville not to bring inspiration, but to gain inspiration from the great movement that has taken place in this community."

Nashville is planning a new and much-needed museum dedicated to its African-American history and culture, which will be located at the corner of Jefferson and 8th Avenues, near the farmer's market. Until this museum is built, the Nashville Public Library is the best place to learn about the city's racially segregated past and the movement that changed that.

NASHVILLE SIT-INS

Greensboro, North Carolina, is often named as the site of the first sit-ins of the American civil rights movement. In truth, activists in Nashville carried out the first "test" sit-ins in late 1959. In these test cases, protesters left the facilities after being refused service and talking to management about the injustice of segregation. In between these test sit-ins and the moment when Nashville activists would launch a full-scale sit-in campaign, students in Greensboro took that famous first step.

The Nashville sit-ins began on February 13, 1960, when a group of African-American students from local colleges and universities sat at a downtown lunch counter and refused to move until they were served. The protesting students endured verbal and physical abuse, and were arrested.

Community members raised money for the students' bail, and black residents of the city began an economic boycott of downtown stores that practiced segregation. On April 19, the home of Z. Alexander Looby, a black lawyer who was representing the students, was bombed. Later the same day, students led a spontaneous, peaceful, and silent march through the streets of downtown Nashville to the courthouse. Diane Nash, a student leader, asked Nashville mayor Ben West if he thought it was morally right for a restaurant to refuse to serve someone based on the color of his or her skin. Mayor West said no.

The march was an important turning point for the city. The combined effect of the sit-ins, the boycott, and the march caused, in 1960, Nashville to be the first major Southern city to experience widespread desegregation of its public facilities. The events also demonstrated to activists in other parts of the South that non-violence was an effective tool of protest.

The story of the young people who led the Nashville sit-ins is told in the book *The Children* by David Halberstam. In 2001, Nashville resident Bill King was so moved by the story of the protests that he established an endowment to fundraise for a permanent civil rights collection at the Nashville Public Library. In 2003, the Civil Rights Room at the Nashville Public Library was opened. It houses books, oral histories, audio-visual records, microfilm, dissertations, and stunning photographs of the events of 1960. The words of one student organizer, John Lewis, who went on to become a congressman from Georgia, are displayed over the entryway: "If not us, then who; if not now, then when?"

The Civil Rights Room is located on the 2nd floor of the library, adjacent to the room that houses its Nashville collection.

The Arcade

One of Nashville's most unique urban features is the covered arcade that runs between 4th and 5th Avenues and parallel to Union Street. The two-story arcade with a gabled glass roof was built in 1903 by developer Daniel Buntin, who was inspired by similar arcades he saw in Italy.

From the moment it opened, the Arcade was a bustling center for commerce. Famous for its peanut shop, the Arcade has also been the location of photo studios, jewelers, and a post office for many years. Today, restaurants crowd the lower level, while professional offices line the 2nd floor.

Downtown Presbyterian Church

William Strickland, the architect who designed the Tennessee State Capitol, also designed the Downtown Presbyterian Church (154 5th Ave. N., 615/254-7584, www.dpchurch.com), a place of worship now on the National Register of Historic Places. Built in 1848 to replace an earlier church destroyed by fire, the church is in the Egyptian revival style that was popular at the time. It is, however, one of only three surviving churches in the country to be built in this style.

Downtown Presbyterian, which added the word "Downtown" to its name in 1955, was used as a Union hospital during the Civil War, and it is where James K. Polk was inaugurated as Tennessee governor in 1839. Visitors are welcome to come for a self-guided tour during regular business hours. Groups of five or more can call in advance for a guided tour of the building.

MUSIC ROW

Home to the business end of the country music industry, Music Row can be found along 16th and 17th Avenues south of where they cross Broadway. While there are few bona fide attractions here, it is worth a jaunt to see the headquarters of both major and independent music labels all in one place.

Music Row's most famous, or infamous, landmark is *Musica,* the sculpture at the Music Row traffic circle. The Alan LeQuire sculpture caused a stir when it was unveiled in 2003 for the larger-than-life anatomically correct men and women it depicts. Regardless of your views on art and obscenity, it is fair to say that *Musica* speaks more to Nashville's identity as the Athens of the South than as Music City USA.

RCA Studio B

As a rule, the music labels in Music Row are open for business, not tours. The lone exception is Historic RCA Studio B (Music Square W., 615/416-2001, www.countrymusichalloffame. com, $12.95). The RCA studio was the second recording studio in Nashville and the place where artists including the Everly Brothers, Roy Orbison, Dolly Parton, Elvis Presley, and Hank Snow recorded hits. Also called the RCA Victor Studio, this nondescript studio operated from 1957 to 1977. Visitors on the one-hour tour, which departs from the Country Music Hall of Fame downtown, hear anecdotes about recording sessions at the studio and see rare footage of a 1960s Dottie West recording session. The studio no longer operates, but it is used in courses at nearby Belmont College.

Tours can only be purchased in conjunction with admission to the Country Music Hall of Fame. Tours depart hourly

Sunday–Thursday 10:30 A.M.–2:30 P.M. On Friday and Saturday, tours leave every half-hour 10:30 A.M.–2:30 P.M.

The Upper Room

Three million Christians around the world know the *Upper Room Daily Devotional Guide,* a page-a-day pocket devotional available in 106 countries and 40 languages. Headquartered in Nashville, the Upper Room Ministry has established a bookstore, museum, and chapel to welcome visitors. **The Upper Room Chapel and Museum** (1908 Grand Ave., 615/340-7207, www.upperroom.org/chapel, Mon.–Fri. 8 A.M.–4:30 P.M., free) features a small museum of Christian-inspired art, including a wonderful collection of nativity scenes from around the world made from materials ranging from needlepoint to camel bone. Visitors may also tour the chapel, with its 8-foot-by-20-foot stained-glass window and 8-foot-by-17-foot wood carving of Leonardo da Vinci's *The Last Supper.* A 15-minute audio presentation discusses features of the carving and tells the history and mission of the Upper Room.

Admission to the Upper Room is free; donations are accepted.

MIDTOWN

Encompassing the neighborhoods of Elliston Place, Hillsboro Village, and Green Hills, midtown refers to the parts of Nashville between downtown and the West End.

◖ The Parthenon

In 1893, efforts began to raise funds for a mighty exposition that would celebrate the 1896 centennial of the state of Tennessee. Though the exposition would start a year late—in 1897—it would exceed all expectations. The old West Side Race Track was converted to a little city, with exhibit halls dedicated to transportation, agriculture, machinery, minerals, forestry, and African Americans, among other themes. There were Chinese, Cuban, and Egyptian villages, a midway, and an auditorium. The exposition attracted 1.7 million people between May 1 and October 31.

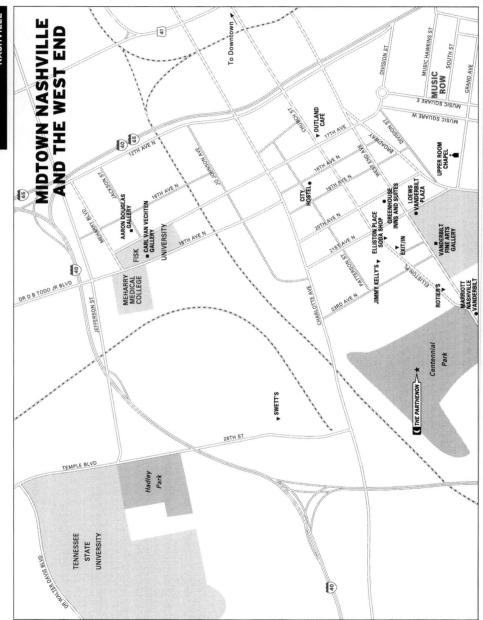

MIDTOWN NASHVILLE AND THE WEST END

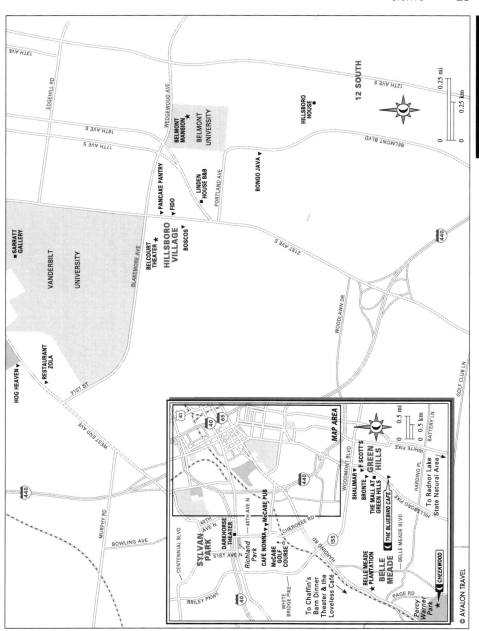

© AVALON TRAVEL

NASHVILLE

© SUSANNA HENIGHAN POTTER

The Parthenon in Centennial Park is one of Nashville's most extraordinary structures.

While the event turned only a modest profit for its organizers, it no doubt contributed in other ways to the local economy and to the stature of the state.

When the exposition closed in the fall of 1897, all the exhibit halls were torn down, except for a life-sized replica of the Greek Parthenon, which had housed an art exhibit during the centennial. The exposition grounds were made into a public park, aptly named Centennial Park, and Nashvillians continued to admire their Parthenon.

The Parthenon replica had been built out of wood and plaster, and it was designed only to last through the centennial. Remarkably, it survived well beyond that. But by the 1920s, the Parthenon was crumbling. City officials, responding to public outcry to save the Parthenon, agreed to restore it, and they hired a contractor to rebuild the replica. The contractor did so using tinted concrete.

Today, the Parthenon remains one of Nashville's most iconic landmarks. It is a monument to the creativity and energy of the New South, and also to Nashville's distinction as the Athens of the South.

You can see and walk around the Parthenon simply by visiting Centennial Park. It is, in many respects, most beautiful from the outside. You can also pay to go inside.

The Parthenon (Centennial Park, 2600 West End Ave., 615/862-8431, Tues.–Sat. 9 A.M.–4:30 P.M., Sun. June–Aug. only 12:30–4:30 P.M., adults $5, seniors and children $2.50) has three gallery spaces; the largest is used to display works from its permanent collection of 63 pieces of American art. The other two galleries host changing exhibits. Visitors to the museum are also able to go inside the Parthenon to view the 42-foot statue of Athena Parthenos.

Belmont Mansion

The elaborate "summer home" of Adelicia Acklen was constructed in 1853 and was named Belle Monte. Belmont Mansion (1900 Belmont Blvd., 615/460-5459, www.belmont-mansion.com, Mon.–Sat. 10 A.M.–4 P.M., Sun.

1–4 P.M., adults $10, seniors $9, children 6–12 $3), as it is known today, is a monument to the excesses of the Victorian age.

Adelicia was born to a wealthy Nashville family in 1817. When she was 22, Adelicia married Isaac Franklin, a wealthy bachelor 28 years her senior. When Franklin died seven years later, Adelicia inherited his substantial wealth. Adelicia remarried to Joseph Acklen, a young lawyer, and together they planned and built Belmont Mansion. The home was built in the Italian style, with touches of Egyptian revival style.

The home boasted 36 rooms and 16,000 square feet of space including a grand gallery where the Acklens hosted elaborate balls and dinner parties. The property included a private art gallery, aviary, zoo, and conservatory, as well as a lake and acres of manicured gardens. After the Civil War, Adelicia traveled to Europe, where she purchased a number of paintings and sculptures that are now on display in her restored mansion.

Shortly before her death, Adelicia sold Belmont to two female educators who ran a girls school from the property for 61 years. Later, it was purchased by the founders of Belmont College, a private college known for its music and music business programs.

Visitors to the mansion are given a 45-minute guided tour of the property, which includes the downstairs sitting and entertaining rooms and three of the upstairs bedrooms.

Vanderbilt University

Named for philanthropist Commodore Cornelius Vanderbilt, who donated $1 million in 1873 to found a university that would "contribute to strengthening the ties which should exist between all sections of our common country," Vanderbilt University (www.vanderbilt.edu) is now one of the region's most respected institutions of higher education.

A private research university, Vanderbilt has an enrollment of 6,300 undergraduates and 5,200 graduates. The university comprises 10 schools, a medical center, public policy center, and The Freedom Forum First Amendment Center. Originally just 75 acres, the university had grown to 250 acres by 1960. When the

McKISSACK AND McKISSACK ARCHITECTS

The oldest African-American architectural firm in Tennessee can trace its roots to Moses McKissack (1790-1865), a member of the West African Ashanti tribe, who was sold into slavery to William McKissack of North Carolina. Later, McKissack moved to Middle Tennessee. Moses became a master builder, and he passed his knowledge on to his son, Gabriel Moses McKissack, born in 1840. Gabriel Moses passed his knowledge of the building trade to his own son, Moses McKissack III, born in 1879.

Moses McKissack III was born in Pulaski, where he received a basic education in the town's segregated schools. In 1890 he was hired by a local white architect. From then until 1905, McKissack designed and built homes throughout the area, including many in Mount Pleasant in Maury County. He devel-

oped a reputation as an excellent architect and tradesman.

In 1905 McKissack moved to Nashville, where he started his own construction company. Within a few years, he was working on major projects. He built a home for the dean of architecture and engineering at Vanderbilt University and the Carnegie Library at Fisk University. In 1922, Moses's brother, Calvin, joined him and they opened McKissack and McKissack, Tennessee's first black architectural firm.

The McKissacks have continued to distinguish themselves in the building industry, and they have also kept the business in the family. Since 1991 the company has been led by Cheryl McKissack, a fifth-generation McKissack. The firm employs more than 100 people and has corporate offices in Philadelphia and New York City.

George Peabody School for Teachers merged with Vanderbilt in 1979, another 53 acres were added.

Vanderbilt's campus life is vibrant, and there is a daily roll call of lectures, recitals, exhibits, and other special events. Check http://calendar.vanderbilt.edu for an up-to-date listing of all campus events.

Prospective students and their parents can sign up for a campus tour. Vanderbilt also offers a self-guided tour of the campus's trees, which form the Vanderbilt Arboretum. Most trees on the tour are native trees common to Nashville and middle Tennessee. This is a nice activity for people who want to hone tree identification skills. Download a podcast or print a paper copy of the tour from the website or contact the university for more information.

Vanderbilt University also has two excellent art galleries: The **Sarratt Gallery** (Sarratt Student Center, Vanderbilt Place near 24th Ave., 615/322-2471, Mon.–Fri. 9 A.M.–9 P.M., Sat.–Sun. 11 A.M.–10 P.M.) has a more contemporary bent than the **Vanderbilt Fine Arts Gallery** (Fine Arts Bldg., Mon.–Fri. noon–4 P.M., Sat.–Sun. 1–5 P.M., free), which includes works that demonstrate the development of both Eastern and Western art, plus six different traveling exhibits annually. The Fine Arts Gallery is located near the intersection of West End and 23rd Avenues. Both galleries are closed or limit their hours during university holidays and semester breaks, so it's a good idea to call ahead.

There is designated visitor parking in several lots on the Vanderbilt campus. Look on the eastern edge of the sports facilities parking lot off Natchez Trace, in the Wesley Place parking lot off Scarritt Place, or in the Terrace Place parking lot between 20th and 21st Avenues north of Broadway.

Belmont University

The school for girls founded in the Belmont Mansion in 1890 evolved in 1913 to the Ward-Belmont School for Women and in 1951 to coed Belmont College. Since 1991, it has been Belmont University, a higher-education institution with links to the Tennessee Baptist Convention. Belmont is a fast-growing university with highly respected music and music business programs. It has a student enrollment of 4,800.

WEST END

Nashville's most posh neighborhood, Belle Meade, is actually a city with its own government. Named after an antebellum plantation, Belle Meade the city is home to Nashville's elite, and famously possesses one of the most wealthy zip codes in America. Drive through to spy on mansions that look more like museums and lawns that look like botanical gardens.

Around Belle Meade are other nice neighborhoods where Nashville's professionals and upper class live. West End Avenue, the area's thoroughfare, is home to lots of nice restaurants. As you head westward, you pass Cheekwood, the Warner Parks, and eventually run into the Natchez Trace Parkway.

Belle Meade Plantation

The mansion at the former Belle Meade Plantation is the centerpiece of present-day Belle Meade Plantation and one of the finest old homes in the city. Its name means "beautiful pasture," and indeed it was Belle Meade's pastures that gave rise to the plantation's fame as the home of a superb stock of horses. Purchased as 250 acres in 1807 by Virginia farmer John Harding and his wife, Susannah, the estate grew to 5,400 acres at its peak in the 1880s and 1890s.

Belle Meade was never a cotton plantation, although small amounts of the cash crop were grown here, along with fruits, vegetables, and tobacco. Instead it was the horses, including the racehorse Iroquois, that made Belle Meade famous. The mansion was built in 1820 and expanded in 1853. Its grand rooms are furnished with period antiques, more than 60 percent of which are original to the house. The estate also includes outbuildings, including a smokehouse, dairy, and the original log cabin that Harding built for his family when they moved to Belle Meade in 1807.

The plantation also includes a slave cabin, which houses an exhibit on Belle Meade's enslaved population, which numbered more than 160 at its peak. Two of these slaves are described in detail. Susanna Carter was the mansion's housekeeper for more than 30 years, and remained with the family even after the end of slavery. On her deathbed, Selena Jackson, the mistress of Belle Meade for many years, called Susanna "one of the most faithful and trusted of my friends." The other African American who features prominently at the museum is Bob Green, whose skill and experience as a hostler earned him one of the highest salaries ever paid to a horse hand of the day.

Visitors to Belle Meade are given a one-hour guided tour of the mansion and then visit the outbuildings and grounds on their own.

◖ Cheekwood

Plan to spend a full morning or afternoon at Cheekwood (1200 Forrest Park Dr., 615/356-8000, www.cheekwood.org, Tues.–Sat. 9:30 A.M.–4:30 P.M., Sun. 11 A.M.–4:30 P.M.,

adults $10, seniors $8, students and children $5) so you can experience the full scope of this magnificent art museum and botanical garden. Galleries in the Cheekwood mansion house the museum's American and European collections, including an excellent contemporary art collection. Cheekwood has the largest public collection of works by Nashville artist William Edmondson, the sculptor and stoneworker. Cheekwood usually displays items from its permanent collection as well as traveling exhibitions from other museums. Many exhibits have special ties with Nashville.

But the Cheekwood is far more than just an art museum. The mansion overlooks hundreds of acres of gardens and woods, and it is easy to forget that you are near a major American city when you're at the Cheekwood. Walk the mile-long Carell Woodland Sculpture Trail past works by 15 internationally acclaimed artists, or stroll past the water garden to the Japanese garden. There are dogwood gardens, an herb garden, a delightful boxwood garden, and much more. Wear comfortable shoes and

© SUSANNA HENIGHAN POTTER

The gardens at Cheekwood are a joy to explore.

NASHVILLE

WILLIAM EDMONDSON

The first African-American artist to have a one-man show at the Museum of Modern Art in New York was Nashville-born sculptor William Edmondson.

Edmondson was born around 1870 in the Hillsboro area of Nashville. He worked for decades as a laborer on the railroads, a janitor at Women's Hospital, and in other similar jobs before discovering his talent for sculpture in 1929. Edmondson told the Nashville *Tennessean* that his talent and passion were God-given: "God appeared at the head of my bed and talked to me, like a natural man, concerning the talent of cutting stone He was about to bestow. He talked so loud He woke me up. He told me He had something for me."

Edmondson was a prolific sculptor. He worked exclusively with limestone, and he created angels, women, doves, turtles, rabbits, and other "varmints." He also made tombstones. Edmondson never learned to read or write, and he called many of his works "mirkels" because they were inspired by God.

In the 1930s, Louise Dahl-Wolfe, a photographer for *Harper's Bazaar* magazine, brought Edmondson and his work to the attention of Alfred Barr, the director of the Museum of Modern Art. Barr and other trustees of the museum admired what they termed as Edmondson's "modern primitive" work, and they invited him to display a one-man show at the museum in 1938. In 1941, the Nashville Art Museum put on an exhibit of Edmondson's work.

Edmondson continued to work until the late 1940s, when he became ill with cancer. He died in 1951 and is buried in an unmarked grave at Mt. Ararat Cemetery in Nashville. The city park at 17th Avenue North and Charlotte Avenue is named in honor of William Edmondson.

You can see an exhibit of Edmondson's work at the Cheekwood Museum.

---

pack a bottle of water so you can enjoy the grounds in comfort.

The Cheekwood owes its existence to the success of the coffee brand Maxwell House. During the 1920s, Leslie Cheek and his wife, Mabel Wood, invested in the new coffee brand being developed by their cousin, Joel Cheek. Maxwell House proved to be a success and earned the Cheeks a fortune, which they used to buy 100 acres of land in West Nashville. The family hired New York residential and landscape architect Bryant Fleming to create a 30,000-square-foot mansion and neighboring gardens. Cheekwood was completed in 1933.

Leslie Cheek lived in the mansion just two years before he died, and Mabel lived there for another decade before deeding it to her daughter and son-in-law, who later offered it as a site for a museum and garden. Cheekwood opened to the public in 1960.

Visitors pay admission at a guard gate at the entrance; there is a total family cap of $30 per car. Once inside, drive to parking lot B so you can explore the art museum and grounds. Parking lot A is for the museum shop and restaurant.

SOUTH NASHVILLE

Head south on 4th Avenue, which becomes Nolensville Pike, towards a diverse array of attractions.

Fort Negley

Early in the Civil War, the Union army determined that taking and holding Nashville was a critical strategic link in their victory. So after Nashville fell in 1862, the Federals wasted no time fortifying the city against attacks. One of the city's forts was Fort Negley, built between August and December 1862 on St. Cloud Hill south of the city center.

Fort Negley owes its existence to the 2,768 men who were enrolled to build it. Most were blacks, some free and some slave, who were pressed into service by the Union army. These men felled trees, hauled earth, and cut and laid limestone for the fort. They slept in the open and enjoyed few, if any, comforts while they labored. Between 600 and 800 men died while building the fort, and only 310 received payment.

When it was completed, Fort Negley was the largest inland masonry fortification in North America. It was never challenged. Fort Negley was abandoned by the military after the war, but it remained the cornerstone of one of Nashville's oldest African-American communities, now known as Cameron-Trimble. During the New Deal, the Works Progress Administration rebuilt large sections of the crumbling fort, and it became a public park.

In 2007, the city opened a visitors center to tell the story of the fort. **Fort Negley Park** (Fort Negley Dr., 615/862-8470, Tues.–Sat. 9 A.M.–4:30 P.M., free) includes a museum about the fort and Nashville's role in the Civil War. There is a short paved loop trail around the base of the fort, plus raised boardwalks through the fortifications themselves. Historic markers tell the story of the fort's construction and detail its military features.

City Cemetery

Right next to Fort Negley Park, off Chestnut Street, is the old City Cemetery. Opened in 1822, City Cemetery (1001 4th Ave. S., www.thenashvillecitycemetery.org) was the final resting place of many of Nashville's most prominent early citizens, including founder James Robertson; William Driver, the U.S. Navy captain who named the flag "Old Glory"; Mabel Lewis Imes and Ella Sheppard, members of the original Fisk Jubilee Singers; and 14 Nashville mayors.

During the Civil War, the cemetery was contracted to bury more than 15,000 Union and Confederate dead, although they were later reinterred in different cemeteries.

Visitors are welcome 8 A.M.–5 P.M. daily. Consult the information board in the Keeble Building for help with your self-guided tour. Guided tours and special events, such as living history tours, garden tours, and historical lectures, take place on the second Saturday of

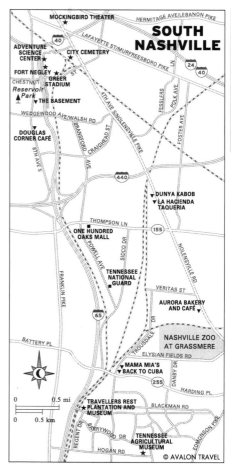

each month. The events are aimed at telling the history of Nashvillians who are buried at this historical cemetery.

Adventure Science Center

Children will enjoy learning about science at the Adventure Science Center (800 Fort Negley Blvd., 615/862-5160, Mon.–Sat. 10 A.M.–5 P.M., Sun. 12:30–5:30 P.M., adults $9, children $7). Interactive exhibits explore how the body works, the solar system, and other scientific

THE BATTLE OF NASHVILLE

During most of the Civil War, Nashville was occupied by Federal forces. After Fort Donelson, 90 miles northeast of Nashville, fell in mid-February 1862, Nashville was in Union hands. The Federals turned Nashville into an important goods depot for the Northern cause, and set strict rules for city residents during occupation.

As the war drew to a close in late 1864, Nashville was the site of what war historians now say was the last major battle of the Western Theater.

The Battle of Nashville came after a string of defeats for the Confederate army of Tennessee, commanded by John Bell Hood. After his bloody and humiliating losses at Spring Hill and Franklin a few miles south, Hood moved north and set up headquarters at Travellers Rest, the home of John Overton. His plan was to set up his troops in an arc around the southern side of the city. Union Maj. Gen. George H. Thomas did not plan to wait for Hood's attack, however. He devised to attack first and drive the Confederates away from Nashville.

A winter storm and frigid temperatures delayed the battle. For two weeks, from December 2 to 14, 1864, the two armies peered at one another across the no-man's-land between the two lines. Then, at dawn on December 15, 1864, the Union attack began. Union troops on foot and horse, including at least four U.S. Colored Infantry brigades, attacked various Confederate posts around the city. By the close of the first day of fighting, Hood withdrew his troops two miles farther south from the city.

The dawn of the second day of battle augured more losses for the Confederates. Unable to hold their line against the Union assault, they fell back again. As darkness fell, Union Maj. Gen. Thomas wired Washington to announce his victory. Pursued by a Union cavalry commanded by Maj. Gen. James Wilson, what remained of the Confederate army of Tennessee marched south and on the day after Christmas crossed the Tennessee River into Alabama. Four months later, the war was over.

An artist depicts the 1864 Battle of Nashville.

areas. The center's new Sudekum Planetarium opened in June 2008. With 164 seats, it is the largest planetarium in Tennessee.

Tennessee Central Railway Museum

Railroad enthusiasts should make a detour to the Tennessee Central Railway Museum (220 Willow St., 615/244-9001, www.tcry.org, Tues., Thurs., and Sat. 9 A.M.–3 P.M., free). This institution is best known for its special railroad excursions (see *Tours* later in this chapter), but they also collect railroad equipment and paraphernalia, which are on display at the museum. The museum is located in an otherwise industrial area between the interstate and the railroad tracks, one block north of Hermitage Avenue and east of Fairfield Avenue.

Nashville Zoo at Grassmere

See familiar and exotic animals at the Nashville Zoo at Grassmere (3777 Nolensville Pike, 615/833-1534, www.nashvillezoo.org, adults $13, seniors $11, children 3–12 $8, children under 3 free). From April 1 to October 15, the zoo is open daily 9 A.M.–6 P.M. The rest of the year, opening hours are daily 9 A.M.–4 P.M. The zoo is closed Thanksgiving, Christmas, and New Year's Days. Parking is free.

Many of the zoo's animals live in beautiful habitats like Lorikeet Landing, Gibbon Islands, and Bamboo Trail. The zoo's meerkat exhibit, featuring the famously quizzical and erect animals, is one of its most popular. The Wild Animal Carousel is an old-time carousel with 39 different brightly painted wooden animals. Two of the newest exhibits feature African wild dogs and Eurasian Lynx.

The zoo is located at Grassmere, the one-time home and farm of the Croft family. The historic Croft farmhouse has been preserved and is open for guided tours in October and December every year.

Travellers Rest Plantation and Museum

Travellers Rest (636 Farrell Pkwy., 615/832-8197, www.travellersrestplantation.org,

Tues.–Sat. 10 A.M.–4 P.M., Sun. 1–4 P.M., $2–10) was the home of John Overton, a Nashville lawyer who helped found Memphis, served on the first Tennessee Supreme Court, and was a trusted advisor to Andrew Jackson, the seventh U.S. president and the first from Tennessee.

Overton was born in Virginia and studied law in Kentucky before he decided to move to Middle Tennessee, what was then the western frontier of the United States. When workmen were digging the cellar for the original home in 1799, they uncovered Native American skeletons and artifacts—Overton had chosen a Mississippian-era Indian mound for the site of his home. But the archaeological finds did not stop Overton, who initially named his home Golgotha, or hill of skulls. The name did not stick, however; tradition has it that Overton later named the home Travellers Rest because it was his place of rest between long trips as a circuit judge in Middle and East Tennessee.

Travellers Rest underwent two major expansions in its lifetime: one in 1808 and another 20 years later. The additions allowed Overton first to accommodate a growing number of young law students who wished to study law with him, later his wife, Mary, and their children, and, finally, the elaborate parties that Overton hosted to further the political career of Andrew Jackson.

John Overton was many different things in his lifetime. Among them was slave owner. Records show that between 30 and 80 slaves lived at Travellers Rest before emancipation. While Overton's plantation was not the primary source of his wealth, it no doubt contributed to his status and prominence. Sadly, when the L&N Railroad purchased the Overton property in the 1940s, the company destroyed not only the Overton family burial ground and peach orchard, but also the slave cabins that remained at the rear of the house.

Visitors to Travellers Rest may choose to skip the mansion tour; admission to the grounds alone is just $3. But to get the full story and flavor of the property, choose the 45-minute guided tour.

Tennessee Agricultural Museum

The Tennessee Agricultural Museum (Ellington Agricultural Center, 615/837-5197, www.tnagmuseum.com, Mon.–Fri. 9 A.M.–4 P.M., free) celebrates the ingenuity and dedicated labors of farm life from the 17th to the 20th century. Operated by the Tennessee Department of Agriculture and set on the department's pleasant south Nashville campus, the museum depicts various facets of Tennessee farm life. There are exhibits about clothes-washing, blacksmithing, coopers, plows, and weaving, just to name a few. Outside, there is a small kitchen garden with heirloom vegetables, and replicas of a log cabin, one-room schoolhouse, and outdoor kitchen. There is also a short self-guided nature trail illustrating the ways that settlers used various types of native Tennessee trees.

Admission to the museum is free, but you can pre-arrange demonstrations for a fee. Staff are also available to answer any questions. This is a good choice for families.

JEFFERSON STREET

Jefferson Street runs from downtown through northwestern Nashville, past several of the city's African-American landmarks.

Bicentennial Mall

Just as Tennessee celebrated its 100th anniversary in 1896 with the construction of Centennial Park, Tennessee celebrated its 200th anniversary in much the same way. The **Bicentennial Capitol Mall State Park** occupies 19 acres on the north side of the capitol building. It offers excellent views of the Capitol, which towers over the mall. The mall and the Capitol are separated by a steep hill and more than 200 steps, which prove daunting to all but the fittest among us.

The mall has dozens of features that celebrate Tennessee and Tennesseans, including a 200-foot granite map of Tennessee embedded in concrete; a River Wall with 31 fountains, each representing one of Tennessee's rivers; and a timeline with Tennessee events, inscriptions,

The Tennessee State Capitol overlooks the Bicentennial Mall, built in 1996 to commemorate Tennessee's 200th anniversary.

THE JUBILEE SINGERS

In 1871, Fisk University needed money. Buildings at the school established in old Union army barracks in 1866 were decaying while more and more African Americans came to seek education.

So, the school choir withdrew all the money from the University's treasury and left on a world tour. The nine singers were Isaac Dickerson, Maggie Porter, Minnie Tate, Jennie Jackson, Benjamin Holmes, Thomas Rutling, Eliza Walker, Green Evans, and Ella Sheppard. Remembering a biblical reference to the Hebrew "year of the jubilee," Fisk treasurer and choir manager George White gave them their name, the Fisk Jubilee Singers.

The singers struggled at first, but before long audiences were praising them. They toured first the American South, then the North, and in 1873 sailed to England for a successful British tour. Their audiences included William Lloyd Garrison, Wendell Phillips, Ulysses S. Grant, William Gladstone, Mark Twain, Johann Strauss, and Queen Victoria. Songs like "Swing Low, Sweet Chariot" and "Nobody Knows the Trouble I've Seen" moved audiences to tears. The singers introduced the spiritual to mainstream white audiences and erased negative misconceptions about African Americans and African-American education.

© SUSANNA HENIGHAN POTTER

Jubilee Hall on the Fisk University campus was paid for by the proceeds of the Fisk Jubilee Singers.

In 1874 the singers returned to Nashville. They had raised enough money to pay off Fisk's debts and build the University's first permanent structure, an imposing Victorian Gothic six-story building now called Jubilee Hall. It was the first permanent structure built solely for the education of African Americans in the United States.

Every October 6, the day in 1871 that the singers departed Fisk, the University recalls their struggle and their triumph with a convocation featuring the modern-day Jubilee Singers.

and notable quotes from 1796 to 1996. There is also a monument to Tennessee's WWII veterans and casualties, and a walk of counties that depicts each of the state's 95 counties. A one-mile path that circles the mall's perimeter is popular with walkers and joggers, and a 2,000-seat amphitheater is used for special events. The park may be a civics lesson incarnate, but it is also a pleasant place to pass the time.

To the west of the mall is the **Nashville Farmer's Market,** where you can buy fresh produce, hot food, and arts and crafts.

Fisk University

Founded in 1866 to educate newly freed slaves, Fisk University (www.fisk.edu) has a long and proud history as one of the United States' foremost black colleges. W. E. B. Du Bois attended Fisk, graduating in 1888, and Booker T. Washington married a Fisk alumna and sent his own children to Fisk. In more modern times, Knoxville native and poet Nikki Giovanni attended Fisk.

Fisk sits at the corner of Jefferson Street and Dr. D. B. Todd Jr. Boulevard, about 10 blocks west of downtown Nashville. The campus is a smattering of elegant redbrick buildings set on open green lawns, although a few more modern buildings, including the library, detract from the classical feel. One of the oldest Fisk buildings is **Jubilee Hall,** on the north

a Fisk University class in 1899

end of the campus, which is said to be the first permanent building constructed for the education of African Americans in the country. It was built with money raised by the Fisk Jubilee Singers, who popularized black spirituals during a world tour from 1871 to 1874. Another notable building is the **Fisk Little Theatre**, a white clapboard building that once served as Union hospital during the Civil War.

At the corner of Jackson Street and Todd Boulevard is the **Carl Van Vechten Gallery,** named for the art collector who convinced artist Georgia O'Keeffe to donate to Fisk a large portion of the work and personal collection of her late husband, Alfred Stieglitz. The college still retains much of this collection, although they have sought to sell parts of it to raise funds for the cash-strapped private school. The legal and financial uncertainty over this art collection has forced the college to put it in storage for the time being. The collection, previously housed at the Van Vechten Gallery, includes works by Stieglitz and O'Keeffe, as well as

acclaimed European and American artists including Pablo Picasso, Paul Cezanne, Pierre-Auguste Renoir, Diego Rivera, Arthur Dove, Gino Severini, and Charles Demuth. It is truly a remarkable collection.

The **Aaron Douglas Gallery** (Jackson St. and 17th Ave. N., Tues.–Fri. 11 A.M.–4 P.M., Sat. 1–4 P.M., Sun. 2–4 P.M., free) houses Fisk's collection of African, African-American, and folk art works. It also hosts visiting exhibits, and others by Fisk students and faculty. It is named after painter and illustrator Aaron Douglas, who also established Fisk's first formal art department. The gallery is located on the top floor of the Fisk library.

Fisk welcomes visitors, but there is no central information desk or printed guide. A map is posted just inside the library, and this is the best place to go to start your visit. Historical markers provide details of each of the main campus buildings. To see the famous painting of the Jubilee Singers, enter Jubilee Hall and bear right to the Appleton Room, where it hangs at the rear.

FISK'S STIEGLITZ COLLECTION

When photographer Alfred Stieglitz died in 1946, his wife, Georgia O'Keeffe, herself one of the most important artists of her generation, was left with the responsibility of giving away his massive art collection. Stieglitz had collected more than 1,000 works by artists including Arthur Dove, Marsden Hartley, O'Keeffe, Charles Demuth, and John Marin. He also owned several African sculptures.

Stieglitz's instructions regarding this art collection were vague. In his will he asked O'Keeffe to select the recipients "under such arrangements as will assure to the public, under reasonable regulations, access thereto to promote the study of art."

O'Keeffe selected several obvious recipients for parts of the collection: the Library of Congress, the National Gallery of Art in Washington, the Metropolitan Museum of Art, the Art Institute of Chicago, and the Philadelphia Museum of Art. Fisk University in Nashville was a surprise, and Carl Van Vechten, a writer, photographer, and friend of Stieglitz and O'Keeffe, is credited with making the suggestion. Van Vechten was keenly interested in African-American art and was close friends with Fisk president Charles Johnson.

O'Keeffe and Fisk were not an easy partnership. According to an account by C. Michael Norton, when she first visited the university a few days before the Carl Van Vechten Gallery would open on campus, O'Keeffe ordered major changes to the gallery space, eventually flying in a lighting designer from New York on the day before the opening. At the opening ceremony on November 4, 1949, held at the Memorial Chapel at Fisk, O'Keeffe declined President Johnson's invitation to the lectern and spoke from her chair, saying curtly: "Dr. Johnson wrote and asked me to speak and I did not answer. I had and have no intention of speaking. These paintings and sculptures are a gift from Stieglitz. They are for the students. I hope you go back and look at them more than once."

The Stieglitz Collection at Fisk consists of 101 works of art, including two by O'Keeffe, 19 Stieglitz photographs, prints by Cezanne and Renoir, and five pieces of African tribal art.

Cash-strapped Fisk has sought to sell parts of the collection to raise funds. A proposal to sell a 50 percent share in the collection for $30 million to Wal-Mart heiress Alice Walton's Crystal Bridges Museum in Bentonville, Arkansas, has been rejected by a court, but Fisk continues to press its case. In 2008, an alternative proposal was made to house the collection in the planned museum of African-American culture, art, and history, to be located near the Bicentennial Mall. But that idea offered no immediate financial relief for Fisk and raised many unanswered questions. Meanwhile, Fisk was ordered to repair the Van Vechten Gallery and again open the collection to the public, or risk losing Stieglitz's bequest altogether.

Meharry Medical College

Just across Dr. D. B. Todd Jr. Boulevard from Fisk is Meharry Medical College, the largest private, comprehensive, historically black institution educating medical professionals. It was founded in 1876 as the Medical Department of the Central Tennessee College of Nashville, under the auspices of the Freeman's Aid Society of the Methodist Episcopal Church.

Meharry was at one time responsible for graduating more than half of all African-American doctors and nurses in the United States. Today it has an enrollment of more than 700 students.

Hadley Park

Founded in 1912, Hadley Park is believed to be the oldest public park developed for African Americans in the South and, most likely, the United States. The park got its start when Fisk University president George Gates requested that the city buy land and create a park for its black citizens. This was in the era of segregation, so other city parks were not open to blacks. The request was granted, and the park opened in July 1912. An old farmhouse was converted into a community center, and benches and a playground were installed. It is now home to a state-of-the-art gym and fitness center, computer labs, meeting rooms, and tennis courts.

Tennessee State University

Founded in 1912 as a normal school for blacks, Tennessee State University (www.tnstate.edu) is now a comprehensive university with more than 9,000 students. In 1979, as a result of a court order to desegregate the state's universities, TSU merged with the Nashville campus of the University of Tennessee. Today, TSU's student body is 75 percent African American.

MUSIC VALLEY

A knot of tourist attractions separated from the rest of Nashville by the Cumberland River, Music Valley has little to recommend it other than the Grand Ole Opry. A strip of motels, restaurants, and dubious country music "museums," this is one tourist zone that you will be just as happy to skip. Unless, of course, you just want to soak up the trashy side of Music City tourism.

If you're game, however, head straight for **Cooter's** (2613 McGavock Pk., 615/872-8358, Mon.–Thurs. 9 A.M.–7 P.M., Fri.–Sat. 9 A.M.–8 P.M., Sun. 9 A.M.–6 P.M., free), a gift shop and museum dedicated to the *Dukes of Hazzard* television show. The museum features a mind-boggling array of toys, ornaments, and model cars manufactured in the 1970s and '80s to profit off the Dukes' wild popularity. You can also see one of the bright-orange Dodge Chargers that became the Dukes' icon. In the gift shop, buy a pair of "official" Daisy Dukes, or any number of General Lee souvenirs. Cooters is operated by Ben Jones who played Cooter, the affable sidekick mechanic, in the original television series. In recent years, Jones has been one of the forces behind DukeFest, a wildly popular annual celebration of fast cars and the General Lee held at the Nashville Motor Speedway.

A few doors down from Cooters, you will find **Willie Nelson and Friends Museum** (2613 McGavock Pike, 615/885-1515, summer daily 9 A.M.–8 P.M., winter daily 9 A.M.–7 P.M.,

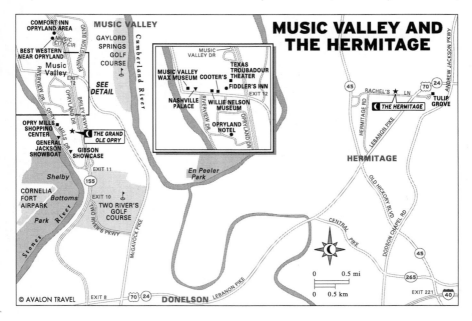

NASHVILLE

$10), which showcases a number of things that once belonged to Willie Nelson, including his golf bag, a replica of his tour bus, and the guitar he played during his first performance on the Grand Ole Opry. Many of the Willie Nelson items were purchased by museum operators Jeannie and Frank Oakley at an IRS auction.

Another choice is the **Music Valley Wax Museum of the Stars** (2515 McGavock Pike, 615/884-7876, daily 9 A.M.–5 P.M., $12), which advertises itself thus: "As close as you can get to Nashville's biggest stars without being slapped with a restraining order." Enough said.

The Grand Ole Opry

Since 1974, the Grand Ole Opry (2802 Opryland Dr., 615/871-6779, www.opry.com) has been performed at the specially built Grand Ole Opry House in Music Valley.

The Opry performs at least two times a week, Friday and Saturday, with additional shows on Tuesday night most weeks. If you don't come to see a show, you can stop at the **Grand Ole Opry Museum** (2802 Opryland Dr., 615/889-6611, Mon., Wed., and Thurs. 10 A.M.–6 P.M., Tues. 10 A.M.–7:30 P.M., Fri. 10 A.M.–8:30 P.M., Sat. 10 A.M.–10 P.M., Sun. noon–5 P.M., free). The museum has exhibits about many early Opry members and performers, including Minnie Pearl and Roy Acuff. It also emphasizes the important link between the Opry and WSM radio, which still broadcasts the Opry live in Nashville and on the Internet. The museum is closed in January and February.

If the Opry isn't occupied with a performance or special event, you can take a backstage tour for $11.

EAST OF NASHVILLE
◖ The Hermitage

Andrew Jackson's plantation and home 16 miles east of Nashville is the area's best historical tourist attraction. The Hermitage (4580 Rachel's Ln., 615/889-2941, www.thehermitage.com, daily 9 A.M.–5 P.M., $7–15, family pass $40) is

The Hermitage was the home of Andrew Jackson, the seventh president of the United States.

OLD HICKORY

Andrew Jackson, the seventh president of the United States, was one of the most important American political figures of the first half of the 19th century. His impact was so great that we now refer to his era as the Age of Jackson and his ideology as Jacksonian Democracy.

Jackson was born in 1767 on the American frontier in South Carolina. His father, an immigrant from Northern Ireland, died before Jackson was born. At age 12, Jackson volunteered for the American army in the Revolutionary War. Jackson's two brothers, Hugh and Robert, died during the war. His mother, Elizabeth, died of smallpox in 1781. Jackson was 14 years old, and alone in the world.

Remarkably, Jackson not only survived; he flourished. In 1784 he moved to Salisbury, North Carolina, where he studied law. In 1787 he became a licensed lawyer and moved west, to Washington County, now part of Tennessee. In 1788 he was appointed the district attorney for the Mero District, now Middle Tennessee.

In Nashville, a city that was founded less than 10 years earlier, Jackson met Rachel Donelson, the daughter of John Donelson. Jackson fell in love with Rachel and in 1781 they were married. Later, when they learned that Rachel's earlier, unhappy marriage to Lewis Robards of Kentucky was not legally dissolved, they remarried in 1794 before a Davidson County justice of the peace.

The Jacksons set about to establish a home and livelihood. Jackson practiced law, speculated in land, and dabbled in politics. They bought farmland in Davidson County where they built the Hermitage, which would be the

Andrew Jackson

COURTESY OF LIBRARY OF CONGRESS/ALEXANDER HAY RITCHIE

Jacksons' home for the rest of their lives. The couple never had children of their own, but they adopted a nephew, who was known as Andrew Jackson Jr., and reared several Indian orphans.

By 1798 Jackson was a circuit-riding judge on the Tennessee Superior Court, but he also developed a reputation for resolving his own conflicts through violence. He brawled with a set of brothers, killed a man in a duel, caned another, and ran a sword through a third. In 1803 he quarreled publicly with governor John Sevier and nearly dueled him as well.

where Jackson retired following his two terms as president of the United States, and it is where he and his beloved wife, Rachel, are buried.

Jackson bought the property in 1809; he and Rachel initially lived in a rustic log cabin, which has since been restored. Jackson first named the home and property Rural Retreat, and later he chose the more poetic name, the Hermitage. Jackson ran a successful cotton plantation on the property, owning as many

as 150 slaves. In 1819 he and Rachel started construction of what is now the mansion. They moved in 1821.

In 1831, two years after he became the nation's seventh president, Jackson expanded the mansion so it was more suitable for presidential entertaining. While Jackson was in Washington, his adopted son, Andrew Jackson Jr., managed the property, and when a chimney fire damaged the house in 1834, Jackson

Jackson's violent temper was better suited for the battlefield. In 1802 he was elected Major General of the Tennessee militia and with the outbreak of war in 1812, his leadership was required. Jackson earned the nickname "Old Hickory" in 1812 when he disobeyed orders and refused to dismiss his Tennessee soldiers in Natchez, Mississippi, marching them back to Tennessee under great hardship instead. He earned national fame three years later when he marched his men from Florida to New Orleans, where he resoundingly defeated the British. The American public was so pleased with their new war hero that they did not mind when they learned the British had actually surrendered two weeks earlier. Neither did they mind some of his tactics: military executions, imposition of martial law, suspension of habeas corpus, and defiance of a federal court order.

In the succeeding years, Jackson fought battles with Native American tribes, and negotiated land treaties with them. By 1821, he quit his post as Major General and came home to the Hermitage for a short retirement.

In 1822 the Tennessee state legislature nominated Jackson for U.S. president and his nomination was seconded by other states. In the 1824 contest, Jackson received more votes than any other contender in the crowded field. But when the U.S. House of Representatives gave the presidency to John Quincy Adams, Jackson called the decision a "corrupt bargain" that violated the will of the voters. His 1828 presidential campaign had begun.

The 1828 campaign was spirited and dirty.

Opponents found seemingly countless stories of Jackson's indiscretions, and they accused him and Rachel of committing adultery by marrying before Rachel's divorce was final. When Rachel Jackson died on December 22, 1828, Jackson accused his opponents of hastening her death by slander.

Jackson was raised as a Presbyterian and held strong religious beliefs throughout his life. He resisted Rachel Jackson's encouragements to formally join a church, however, saying that he feared the charge of hypocrisy that could be leveled against him as a public churchgoer. Jackson promised Rachel that when he left public life he would join the church, and he was true to his word. In July 1838, Jackson, then in his 70s, joined the church.

During his two terms as president, Jackson enraged his opponents and delighted supporters. He took unprecedented actions in the name of reform, including several controversial banking decisions. He believed in a strong federal government and stood in the way of state nullification of federal laws. By the end of his eight years in the White House, Jackson was known by his opponents as "King Andrew," while his supporters still saw him as a spokesman of the common man.

Jackson, who never remarried, spent the remaining eight years of his life at the Hermitage, where he entertained guests, helped to manage the farm, and dispensed advice to politicians. His health declined, though, and in 1845, at age 78, he died and was buried in the Hermitage garden, next to his beloved Rachel.

Jr. and his wife, Sarah, saw to its restoration. At the end of Jackson's second term in office in 1837, he retired to the Hermitage and lived here happily until his death in 1845.

Following President Jackson's death, the Hermitage remained in family hands until 1853, when it was sold to the State of Tennessee to pay off the family's debts. It opened as a museum in 1889 and was restored largely due to the persistence of the Ladies Hermitage

Association. Because the property never left family hands before it was sold to the State, many of the furnishings are original and even the wallpaper in several rooms dates back to the years when Andrew Jackson called it home.

One major strength of the present-day Hermitage tour and museum is that it focuses not only on Jackson and the construction and decoration of the mansion, but also the African-American slaves who worked at the

Hermitage plantation. Curators and archaeologists have studied the Hermitage to learn about the hundreds of men and women who made the Hermitage profitable and successful for so many years. The tour of the grounds takes visitors to Alfred's Cabin, a slave cabin occupied until 1901 by former Hermitage slave Alfred Jackson. You also learn about the agriculture that took place on the Hermitage, and can see cotton being cultivated during the summer months. To learn even more about the Hermitage's slaves, take an add-on wagon tour, offered from April to October.

Visitors to the Hermitage begin with a video about Andrew Jackson and the Hermitage, and can continue on to a museum. You take an audio tour of the grounds, and guided tours are offered of the mansion. You wind up in the gift shop and café. Plan on spending at least three hours here to make the most of your visit. Try to come when the weather is good.

TOURS
Nash Trash Tours
Nashville's most notorious tour guides are Sheri Lynn and Brenda Kay Jugg, sisters who ferry thrill-seekers around Nashville in a big pink school bus. The Nash Trash Tour (615/226-7300 or 800/342-2123, www.nashtrash.com, $30) is a raunchy, rollicking, rib-tickling tour of city attractions, some of which you won't even find in this guidebook. Be prepared to be the butt of some of the jokes yourself; their "I Got Trashed" T-shirts have a double meaning. You'll snack on canned cheese and there's a pit stop to buy beer. Not appropriate for children or adults who aren't comfortable laughing at themselves and others. As Sheri Lynn says: "If we haven't offended you, just give us some time."

Gray Line Tours
Nashville's largest tour company, Gray Line (2416 Music Valley Dr., 615/883-5555 or

800/251-1864), offers no fewer than 12 different sightseeing tours of the city. The three-hour Discover Nashville tour costs $40 per adult and includes entrance to the Ryman Auditorium, the Country Music Hall of Fame, and stops at other city landmarks.

The three-hour Homes of the Stars tour takes you past the homes of stars including Alan Jackson, Vince Gill, Dolly Parton, and the late Tammy Wynette for $35. There is also a one-hour downtown trolley tour for $12 and a 90-minute downtown walking tour for $20.

General Jackson Showboat
Enjoy lunch or dinner, live entertainment, and a cruise along the Cumberland on the General Jackson Showboat (2812 Opryland Dr., 615/458-3900, www.generaljackson.com). Midday tickets range $30–50 and include lunch. Evening tickets are $35–90 and include a three-course dinner. You can cruise and skip the meal at midday or in the evening for $17.

Tennessee Central Railway
The Tennessee Central Railway Museum (220 Willow St., 615/244-9001, www.tcry.org) offers an annual calendar of sightseeing and themed railway rides in central Tennessee. Excursions include fall foliage tours, Christmas shopping expeditions, and trips to scenic small towns. All trips run on the Nashville and Eastern Railroad, which runs east, stopping in Lebanon, Watertown, and Cookville, and terminates in Monterrey.

Trips sell out early, so book your tickets well in advance.

Nashville Black Heritage Tours
Call ahead to book a tour for your family or group with Bill Daniel of Nashville Black Heritage Tours (5188 Almaville Rd., Smyrna, 615/890-8153), who will craft a tour of the city's most important African-American heritage sites.

Entertainment

From shopping to live music, Nashville offers visitors plenty of diversions. Even if you are not a fan of country music, you will find plenty to do in Music City.

LIVE MUSIC AND CLUBS

No trip to Nashville is complete without listening to some live music. Music City overflows with musicians and opportunities to hear them. So whether you catch a show at the Opry, stake out a seat at the Bluebird Cafe, or enjoy a night at the symphony, be sure to make time for music during your visit.

Even before you arrive in the city, you can plan out your nights thanks to the Nashville Convention and Visitors Bureau (www.nashvillecvb.com). Through a handy feature on the bureau's website you can check out upcoming concerts a month or more in advance. Many venues will let you buy tickets in advance over the phone or online.

Published on Wednesday, the *Nashville Scene* always includes detailed entertainment listings and recommendations. The *Tennessean,* the city's daily paper, publishes its entertainment insert on Friday.

◖ The Grand Ole Opry

If there's anything you really must do while in Nashville, it's go to see the Grand Ole Opry (2802 Opryland Dr., 615/871-6779 or 800/733-6779, www.opry.com, $35–50). For more than 80 years this weekly radio showcase of country music has drawn crowds to Nashville. Every show at the Opry is still broadcast live on WSM, a Nashville AM radio station. Shows are also streamed online and some are televised on cable. But nothing quite beats being there.

The Opry runs on Friday and Saturday night, with two two-and-a-half-hour shows each night. The early show starts at 6:30 P.M. and the late show starts at 9:30 P.M. Sometimes there is a bonus show on Tuesday evening.

Since this is a radio broadcast, shows start and end right on time.

Every Opry show is divided into 30-minute segments, each of which is hosted by a different member of the Opry. This elite country music fraternity includes dozens of stars that you've heard of and others you haven't. The host performs two songs; one at the beginning of their half-hour segment and one at the end. In between they will introduce two or three other performers, each of whom will sing about two songs. In between segments, the announcers read radio commercials and stagehands change around the stage set.

All in all, it is a fast-paced show that keeps your toes tapping. Even if there's an act that you don't like, they won't be on the stage for too long. Of course, the flip side is that if it's an act you love, well, they're only on the stage for two songs too. Even when the biggest stars appear on the Opry stage, they rarely sing more than a few numbers.

The Opry usually releases the full line-up for each show about a week in advance. Some fans wait until then to buy their tickets so they're sure to catch a big-name artist. My advice is to forget about bragging to your friends back home about who you saw at the Opry and buy tickets to any show at all. Each show is carefully balanced to include bluegrass, classic country, popular country, and, sometimes, gospel. It is a true showcase that every fan of country music will enjoy.

Most Opry shows take place in the Grand Ole Opry House, a 4,400-seat auditorium in Music Valley. The interior of the hall was designed to look like the Ryman Auditorium, although the seats are much more comfortable. A circle of the original stage from the Ryman was cut out and placed in the center of the Opry House stage, and it is here that artists stand when they perform. Several months out of the year the Opry returns to the Ryman for its Opry at the Ryman season.

THE GRAND OLE OPRY

Nashville's most famous broadcast can trace its roots to October 1925, when Nashville-based National Life and Accident Insurance Company opened a radio station in town. Its call letters, WSM, stood for "We Shield Millions," the company's motto.

WSM hired George D. Hay, a radio announcer who had worked in Memphis and Chicago, to manage the station. Hay – who, while in Chicago, had announced one of the nation's first live country radio shows – planned to create a similar such program in Nashville.

On November 25, 1925, Hay invited a 78-year-old fiddler, Uncle Jimmy Thompson, to perform live on Saturday night over the radio waves. The response was electric, and WSM continued to broadcast live old-time music every Saturday night. In May 1927, the program developed the name the Grand Ole Opry, practically by chance. An announcer named Judge Hay was segueing from the previous program of classical opera to the barn dance. "For the past hour, we have been listening to music taken largely from Grand Opera. From now on, we will present the Grand Ole Opry," he said. The name stuck.

During the first few years, most Opry performers were unknowns who worked day jobs in and around Nashville. But as the show gained in popularity, some acts were able to make it professionally, including Uncle Dave Macon, the Vagabonds, and the Delmore Brothers. By 1939, the Opry gained a slot on the nationwide NBC radio network, allowing it to reach a national audience every week.

Always a live audience show, the Opry was performed in several different venues over the years. It started in the WSM studio, then moved to the Hillsboro Theater (now the Belcourt), the Dixie Tabernacle on Fatherland Street, and the War Memorial Auditorium downtown. In 1943 it moved to the Ryman Auditorium, where it remained until 1974, when National Life built a new 5,000-seat auditorium in a rural area north of Nashville. The first show from the new Opry House in Music Valley was broadcast on March 16, 1974. President Richard Nixon attended. In 1983, the Opry was acquired by Oklahoma-based Gaylord Broadcasting Company. The Opry is still owned by Gaylord Entertainment.

The music that flows from the Opry's stage on a Saturday night (and now, Tuesday and Friday too) has changed since the first fiddler took the airwaves. Just as country music broadened its appeal by softening its hard edges, the Opry has evolved with its audience. Today it is a showcase for all types of country and country-inspired music, including bluegrass, gospel, honky-tonk, and zydeco. It remains, however, one of the most esteemed and celebrated institutions in country music.

COURTESY THE TENNESSEE DEPT. OF TOURIST DEVELOPMENT

The Opry is the most famous stage in country music.

Ernest Tubb Midnite Jamboree

Texas Troubadour Ernest Tubb started a tradition when he set up a live radio show at the back of his Broadway record shop. The show was broadcast after the Opry shut down across the street, and it lived up to its name, the Midnite Jamboree. The Jamboree continues, now broadcast from the **Texas Troubadour Theatre** (Music Valley Village, 2416 Music Valley Dr., 615/889-2472, www.ernesttubb. com, no cover). Located across the street from the Opryland Hotel, the Jamboree gets started early in the evening, while the Opry is still on, but things really get swinging after midnight.

The Texas Troubadour Theatre is also home to the **Cowboy Church** (2416 Music Valley Dr., 615/859-1001, www.nashvillecowboychurch. org). Every Sunday morning at 10 A.M., locals and tourists dressed in anything from shorts to Stetsons gather here for a lively praise-and-worship country gospel church service led by Dr. Harry Yates and Dr. Joanne Cash Yates. The church was founded in 1990 with just six souls; today it attracts hundreds to its weekly services. Country and gospel music legends make cameo performances now and again, but the real star is Jesus.

The Gibson Showcase

Guitar manufacturer Gibson has a concert venue next to its Nashville retail store. The Gibson Showcase (161 Opry Mills Dr., 615/514-2200, ext. 231, cover varies) puts on weekday bluegrass concerts, evening dinner events, and special shows. Bluegrass jams start at 8 P.M. on Monday nights; there's no cover charge and reservations are not accepted. Just Country and More is a showcase of country music classics, pop tunes, and family entertainment performed while guests chow on a Southern dinner menu. Special events include performances by jazz, blues, bluegrass, and country greats.

The Ryman Auditorium

The most famous music venue in Nashville, the Ryman Auditorium (116 5th Ave. N., www. ryman.com, cover varies) continues to book some of the best acts in town, of just about every genre you can imagine. On the good side, the hall still boasts some of the best acoustics around. On the bad, the bench seats are just as uncomfortable as ever. But if the show is good, you probably won't even notice.

Country Music Hall of Fame

The Country Music Hall of Fame (222 5th Ave. S., 615/416-2100, www.countrymusic-halloffame.com) hosts concerts, readings, and musical discussions regularly in an auditorium located inside the hall. These daytime events are often aimed at highlighting one type of country music or another, but sometimes you'll find big names playing. Admission is free with your paid admission to the hall, so it is a good idea to plan your trip to the hall on a day when there's a concert scheduled (separate admission to concerts is not available). Check the website for a listing of upcoming events.

❏ The Bluebird Cafe

For a certain type of music fan, the Bluebird Cafe (4104 Hillsboro Pike, 615/383-1461, www.bluebirdcafe.com, cover varies) has a whole lot going for it. It is intimate and homey. It books some of the best up-and-coming country and acoustic acts in the business. Its shows start as early as 6:30 P.M. There's no smoking, no talking during the acts, and virtually none of the usual bar pick-up scene. In short, the Bluebird is a place where music comes first, and everything else is a far second.

Opened in 1982 by Amy Kurland, the Bluebird started out as a casual restaurant with live music. It's located next to a dry cleaners in a nondescript shopping mall a few miles south of Hillsboro Village. Over the years, it has evolved into a destination for music lovers who appreciate its no-nonsense take on live music, and who hope that they just might stumble in on the next big thing. The Bluebird is famous as an early venue for the then-unknown Garth Brooks, but its stage has also hosted the likes of Emmylou Harris, Kathy Mattea, Gillian Welch, Trisha Yearwood, and Steve Earle, among many more.

The Bluebird Cafe hosts intimate concerts and open mics.

The Bluebird opens every night of the week, and most evenings the entertainment starts at 6:30 P.M. Cover is usually under $10. There is no cover charge and no reservations accepted for the shows on Sunday, songwriters' night, or Monday, open-mic night, but guests should arrive by 5:30 P.M. to get one of the first-come, first-served seats. There are only 21 tables and a few additional seats at the bar, so you have to be on your toes to get a spot in the house. For shows on Friday and Saturday nights, the Bluebird takes reservations the Monday of that week noon–5 P.M. Be advised that many weeks the shows sell out in a mere half hour, so keep hitting that redial button! Reservations for Tuesday–Thursday shows are available a week ahead 11 A.M.–5 P.M. You can also make reservations online. There is a $7 minimum per seat at all shows, so come hungry or thirsty. The food is standard bar fare, nothing more and nothing less. No outside drinks are allowed.

Once you've successfully navigated the rules of getting a seat at the Bluebird, sit back and enjoy some fine live music. Nashville is the city where anybody can become a somebody, and it's places like the Bluebird that make that happen. Be a part of it.

Clubs

If there is one false assumption that many people have about Nashville, it is that this is a strictly country town. In fact, Nashville has a vibrant rock 'n' roll music scene, plus good blues and jazz. So in a city where country music rubs shoulders with great rock, blues, and Americana, most live music venues refuse to be pigeonholed.

Venues here are categorized by their predominant music type, but keep in mind that variety is the name of the game. Most bars and clubs charge a cover when there is a band or performer, while songwriter nights and open mics are usually free.

COUNTRY

Nashville's most colorful country music establishments are the honky-tonks that line Broadway. Once places where country boys and girls would come to shake a leg or meet a beau, these all-day, all-night bars and music clubs now cater to visitors. **Tootsie's Orchid Lounge** (422 Broadway, 615/726-0463, no cover) is painted purple and exudes classic country every day of the week beginning as early as 10 A.M. Three doors down from Tootsie's is **Robert's Western World** (416 Broadway, 615/244-9552, no cover), voted the city's best honky-tonk. Originally a store selling boots, cowboy hats, and other country music regalia, Roberts morphed into a bar and nightclub with a good gift shop. Another choice is **The Stage** (412 Broadway, 615/726-0504, no cover), with a large dance floor and music seven nights a week.

After the Opry moved to Music Valley in the late 1970s, taking with it the customers who kept Broadway businesses afloat, the street's honky-tonks subsisted first on local bar flies and later on the tourist trade. Whether you're looking for a place to drown your sorrows or kick off a night on the town, Broadway's honky-tonks are a good place to go.

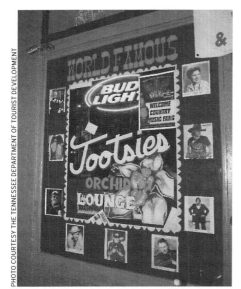

Tootsie's Orchid Lounge on Broadway is Nashville's most famous honky-tonk.

Probably the most popular country music nightclub downtown, the **Wildhorse Saloon** (120 2nd Ave. N., 615/902-8200, www.wildhorsesaloon.com, cover varies) is a boot-scootin' and beer-drinking place to see and be seen. When the Wildhorse opened in 1994, promoters drove a herd of cattle through the streets of downtown Nashville. Today, the Wildhorse is still a place where a good show and a good time are the top priorities. The huge dance floor is often packed with cowboys and cowgirls line dancing to the greatest hits of the country music genre. Dance lessons are offered every day (Mon.–Thurs. 6:30–8:30 P.M., Fri. 6–9:30 P.M., Sat. noon–9:30 P.M., Sun. 2–7:30 P.M.). The Wildhorse books big-name acts many nights of the week, including country music, roots rock, and classic rock stars. The Wildhorse opens Thursday through Sunday at 11 A.M., and on Monday at 5 P.M. When there is a show on, doors normally close at 6 P.M. and re-open at 7 P.M. for people with tickets. On other nights the cover charge ranges $4–6. From 10 P.M. on, the Wildhorse is a 21-and-up club.

The city's most popular venue for bluegrass and roots music, **The Station Inn** (402 12th Ave. S., 615/255-3307, cover varies) showcases fine artists every night of the week. This homey and casual club opens nightly at 7 P.M., with music starting about 9 P.M. This is a 21-and-over club, unless you come with a parent or guardian. There is no cover for the Sunday-night bluegrass jam.

The **Douglas Corner Cafe** (2106-A 8th Ave. S., 615/298-1688, cover varies) offers a Tuesday-night open mic, and country acts the rest of the week. It is known as a place where singer-songwriters are discovered, and it is not unlike the Bluebird Cafe in attitude and ambience. An intimate setting, full menu, and good acoustics make this a popular choice for music listening. Several live albums have been recorded here.

The **Nashville Palace** (2400 Music Valley Dr., 615/889-1540, no cover) is a restaurant, nightclub, and dance floor across from the Opryland Hotel. Live music is on tap daily starting at 5 P.M., and talent nights on Tuesday and Wednesday always draw a crowd.

JAZZ AND BLUES

If you need to get that country twang out of your head, a good dose of the blues will do it. **B. B. King Blues Club** (152 2nd Ave. N., 615/256-2727, cover varies) is a good place to start for a night of the blues. The club is a satellite of King's original Beale Street club, and it books live blues every night. The cover charge is usually under $10, unless B. B. King himself is making one of his rare appearances.

In Printer's Alley, the **Bourbon Street Blues and Boogie Bar** (220 Printer's Alley, 615/242-5867, cover varies) is a hole-in-the-wall nightclub that specializes in New Orleans–style jazz and blues.

A fine dining restaurant next door to Green Hills Mall, **F. Scott's** (2210 Crestmore Rd., 615/269-5861, no cover) is also the city's premier venue for live jazz. The music goes well with the restaurant's art deco appeal. Come for dinner or for a few drinks at the bar while you listen in. Although there's no cover at the door, there is a two-drink minimum if you're not dining.

ECLECTIC

Clubs listed here may book a rock band one night and folk the next. Always check the free weekly *Nashville Scene* for the latest entertainment listings.

12th and Porter (114 12th Ave. S., 615/254-7250, cover varies) is a favorite venue for live music in the city. Second only to the Ryman in popularity, 12th and Porter books all kinds of acts. They are a popular choice for music-label showcases, and legendary performers have been known to stage impromptu shows here. Spacious and offering a full menu, including good Mexican food, 12th and Porter is a great hangout and place to hear live music.

The **Exit/In** (2208 Elliston Pl., 615/321-3340, cover varies) has been a favorite rock music venue for years, although it also books alternative country, blues, and reggae. Located on Elliston Place, the club is convenient to Vanderbilt and downtown.

Coffee shop by day, bar and live music venue by night, **Café Coco** (210 Louise Ave., 615/321-2626, cover varies) in Elliston Place is the best of both worlds. Monday is songwriter's night, Tuesday is open-mic poetry, and Thursday is open-mic music. Jazz and rock bands play other nights, when the cover ranges $2–5.

The Basement (1604 8th Ave. S., 615/254-8006, www.thebasementnashville.com, cover varies) calls itself a cellar full of noise, but it's a good kind of noise. Indie rock is the most common art form here, but they book other types of acts too. The Basement's New Faces Night on Tuesday is a popular place to hear singer-songwriters. Admission is 21 and over, unless accompanied by a parent or guardian. There is a full bar and light menu. Note that inside the club is totally smoke-free; there is an outdoor smoking porch. The brick walls and subterranean feel give the Basement its cool atmosphere. Park behind the club and on side streets.

Located in an old warehouse that has housed a flour mill, jam factory, and country music concert hall, **Cannery Row** (One Cannery Row, 615/251-3020, www.mercy-lounge.com, cover varies) and its derivative **Mercy Lounge** are two cool venues for live music. Cannery Row is a large, somewhat cavernous space with lots of nice cherry-red touches, hardwood floors, and a shiny red bar. It can hold up to 1,000 people. The Mercy Lounge upstairs is a bit more intimate, with a capacity of up to 500 people. The Mercy Lounge hosts 8 off 8th on Monday nights, an open mic where eight different bands get to perform three songs. Both venues book rock, country, soul, and all sorts of other acts. It is located off 8th Avenue South.

A music venue designed by performers, **The Rutledge** (410 4th Ave. S., 615/782-6858, www.therutledgelmv.com, cover varies) has some of the most ear-pleasing acoustics in the city. An intimate venue—it seats only 250—the Rutledge books a wide variety of acts, hosts industry events, and even puts on tribute shows now and then. It is a smoke-free club and serves a limited food menu.

3rd and Lindsley (818 3rd Ave. S., 615/259-

9891, www.3rdandlindsley.com, cover varies) is a neighborhood bar and grill that showcases rock, alternative, progressive, Americana, soul, and R&B music. Over the years they have developed a reputation for booking good blues acts. They serve a full lunch and dinner menu, the bar is well-stocked, and the club offers a great atmosphere and sound quality. Smoking is allowed.

Over in East Nashville, the **French Quarter Cafe** (823 Woodland St., 615/227-3100, cover varies) offers a Thursday night in-the-round songwriter's night. Weekends will find blues, rock, and soul musicians on the stage at this New Orleans–style nightclub. Dine on spicy po-boys, muffaletta, or other Cajun specialties while you enjoy a night out.

CONCERT SERIES

Dyer Observatory (1000 Oman Dr., 615/373-4897, www.dyer.vanderbilt.edu), a working space observatory operated by Vanderbilt University, has emerged as a popular venue for music, thanks to two ongoing concert series. **Music on the Mountain,** with Blair School of Music, and **Bluebird on the Mountain,** with the Bluebird Cafe, bring live music to this dramatic and one-of-a-kind spot. Imagine a night of fine music enjoyed under the stars, with the fresh air and the atmosphere of the forest all around you.

Every October the Grand Ole Opry celebrates its birthday with **Opry Month,** four weeks of star-studded performances, including several at the Opry's original home, the Ryman Auditorium. Get your tickets early, since these shows are always popular.

Also taking place on Thursday nights in the summer, **Bluegrass Nights at the Ryman** is a concert series that features some of the best pickers in the country. Starting in June and ending in July, this Ryman Auditorium series is always popular.

For a laid-back evening in a one-of-a-kind setting, check out the Tennessee Jazz and Blues Society's concert series **Jazz on the Lawn** (www.jazzblues.org). On Sunday evenings from May to October, jazz and blues artists take the stage on the lawns of some of Nashville's most historic homes, including the Hermitage, Belle Meade, and Cheekwood. Bring your own picnic and blanket.

BARS

Bar-hopping is best enjoyed downtown, where there is the greatest concentration of nightclubs, restaurants, and bars. Even on weeknights, the District, which lies along lower Broadway and its side streets, is crowded with people dressed in designer cowboy boots and fringed shirts. This is the official entertainment district of Nashville, and it is well-patrolled by police and cruisers alike.

Outside of the District, there are several other enclaves of nightlife that cater more to residents than visitors.

Nashville won't issue a liquor license unless the establishment also serves food, so all of the bars listed below double as restaurants.

The District

The honky-tonks along Broadway, Wildhorse Saloon, and B. B. King Blues Clubs are several of the most popular nightclubs in the District. Right next to the Wildhorse Saloon in the heart of the District, **Coyote Ugly** (154 2nd Ave. N., 615/254-8459, www.coyoteugly.com) draws a youthful, raucous crowd. Drinking beer and making friends are the two primary pursuits here, and for many people, there's no better place to do either.

Memorabilia of Nashville's past adorns the walls at **Legends Corner** (428 Broadway, 615/248-6334), a popular club for live music and rollicking crowds. There is never a cover, but be sure to put in a few bucks when they pass the hat for the performer.

Farther afield, but still downtown, you'll find one of the city's best beer bars. Behind the Union Station Hotel on the west side of downtown, the **Flying Saucer** (1001 Broadway, 615/259-7468) has one of the best selections of beer in town. Monday is pint night, when you can get $2.50 pints of just about any of the beers on the wall.

Duck into **The Beer Sellar** (107 Church St.,

615/254-9464) to experience its "50 draughts, 150 bottles and 1 bitching jukebox." Located within walking distance of downtown, this is a cozy bar for conversation and fun.

Another popular brewpub is **Big River Grille and Brewing Works** (111 Broadway, 615/251-4677), an imposing bar and restaurant in the heart of the District. They serve food as well as boutique beers from around the world.

Printer's Alley

This narrow patch of downtown, located in between 3rd and 4th Avenues off Church Street, is home to a half-dozen nightclubs and bars, many that cultivate a seedy reputation. While reality may be a bit more tame, it is still a popular place to let loose. Elaborate wrought-iron balconies and the cobblestone underfoot evoke Bourbon Street, a parallel that seems to suit the place. Bars here include **Bourbon Street Blues and Boogie Bar** (220 Printer's Alley, 615/242-5867) and **Fiddle and Steel** (201 Printer's Alley, 615/251-9002). Printer's Alley also has a karaoke bar and one of the city's most storied adult-entertainment bars.

Midtown

Elliston Place is home to several live music clubs plus a few neighborhood bars. The Exit/In and The End have live bands most nights of the week. You can play a game of pool at **Elliston's Pool Place Hall** (2200 Elliston Pl., 615/320-9441). This is a back-to-the-basics hangout where good drinks, good pool, and good people make for a good night out. **The Gold Rush** (2205 Elliston Pl., 615/321-1160) is a popular late-night mellow hangout. Finally, **Sherlock Holmes' Pub** (2206 Elliston Pl., 615/327-1047), which models itself as an old-fashioned English pub, has fish-and-chips and pints of beer.

Also an upscale restaurant, **Virago** (1811 Division St., 615/320-5149) in Music Row is a trendy bar and late-night pit stop. The S-shaped bar is the perfect place to order a martini and imagine you're in a big city.

Boscos (1805 21st Ave. S., 615/385-0050)

calls itself a beer-lover's restaurant. While food is important here, it is Boscos' reputation for good beer that keeps patrons coming back. Stake out a front window seat to people-watch in trendy Hillsboro Village while you drink your beer.

Also in Hillsboro Village, **Cabana** (1910 Belcourt Ave., 615/577-2262) is a popular place to people-watch and unwind. It is a bar/restaurant/late-night hangout that attracts a youthful and well-dressed crowd. Lounge at the bar or in the expansive backyard. Choose from dozens of beers, wines, and some excellent martinis.

In the Green Hills area, **The Greenhouse** (2211 Bandywood Dr., 615/385-3357) offers specialty drinks, beers, and lots of hanging plants. To find it, look for the Green Hills Kroger and take a left. A few doors down, **The Box Seat** (2221 Bandywood Dr., 615/383-8018) is a bona fide sports bar with televisions in every direction.

South Street Original Crab Shack and Authentic Dive Bar (907 20th Ave. S., 615/320-5555) is an institution, serving Cajun specialties and a relaxed atmosphere. Head upstairs to the open-air Treehouse, perfect for a warm Nashville night.

Broadway Brewhouse (1900 Broadway, 615/340-0089) has more than 70 different beers on tap and 100 more in coolers.

East Nashville

Edgefield Sports Bar and Grille (921 Woodland St., 615/228-6422) is a no-frills watering hole that caters to East Nashville residents.

The Family Wash (2038 Greenwood Ave., 615/226-6070) is a live music listening room where people come for a pint of beer and food too. It's also a neighborhood joint for the up-and-coming East Nashville community.

For a fun, retro vibe and a dance floor that gets hopping most nights of the week, grab a table at the **Alleycat Lounge** (1008-B Woodland St., 615/262-5888).

You might think you're in Austin at the **Rosepepper Cantina** (1907 Eastland Ave., 615/227-4777), a Mexican restaurant and bar.

Choose from 30 different variations on the margarita, and enjoy the house band on weekend nights.

12 South

The up-and-coming neighborhood on 12th Avenue South is attracting new residents and businesses. Here you can enjoy a martini at **Mirror** (2317 12th Ave. S., 615/383-8330), a Miami Beach–inspired restaurant and bar. Enjoy the tapas menu while you sip your drink and people-watch.

Snag a seat on the crowded patio outside **Mafiaoza's Pizzeria and Neighborhood Pub** (2400 12th Ave. S., 615/269-4646, www.mafiaozas.com), a popular neighborhood hangout known for its top-notch pizza.

For something a little different, head to **Rumors Wine and Art Bar** (2304 12th Ave. S., 615/292-9400), a homey wine bar and art gallery. Good for wine lovers and aspiring wine lovers alike, this is a popular place for residents of the trendy 12 South district to get together. Rumors has a satellite location in East Nashville, at 112 Woodland Street (615/262-5346).

GAY AND LESBIAN NIGHTLIFE

You don't have to be gay to enjoy **Tribe** (1517-A Church St., 615/329-2912), but it helps to be beautiful, or at least well-dressed. The dance floor here is one of the best in the city, and the atmosphere is hip. Martinis and other specialty drinks are the poison of choice at this standard-setting club, which stays open until the wee hours.

Right next door to Tribe is **Play** (1519 Church St., 615/322-9627), the city's newest gay club, with drag shows and performances by adult-film stars.

The Chute Complex (2535 Franklin Rd., 615/297-4571) has karaoke, drag shows, and a dance floor. It caters to gay men.

Women outnumber men at the **Lipstick Lounge** (1400 Woodland St., 615/226-6343), a cool yet homey club in East Nashville. Live music, pool, and great food attract a crowd nearly every night.

For a low-key evening of pool or a happy hour stop before dinner, **TRAX** (1501 2nd Ave. S., 615/742-8856) is the place to go. The patio is a nice place to sit in warm weather. There is wireless Internet and big-screen televisions.

Outloud Cafe (1707 Church St., 615/329-8006) is a casual restaurant, coffee shop, and low-key venue for entertainment, catering to the gay and lesbian crowd. Thursday is movie night, there are monthly art exhibits, and game night is Monday beginning at 7 P.M.

COMEDY

Nashville's only comedy club is **Zanies** (2025 8th Ave. S., 615/269-0221), where you can hear stand-up comics every weekend and some weeknights.

THE ARTS

Before Nashville was Music City, it was the Athens of the South, a city renowned for its cultural, academic, and artistic life. Universities, museums, and public arts facilities created an environment for artistic expression unparalleled by any other Southern city.

These days, most people think that country music is Nashville's only art form. But the truth is that Nashville offers far more than honkytonks and the Opry. It has an opera company of its own, not to mention an award-winning symphony, buoyant arts scene, and ample opportunities to sample contemporary and classic music, film, and theater.

Theater

The **Tennessee Repertory Theatre** (505 Deaderick St., 615/782-4000, www.tennesseerep.org) is Tennessee's largest professional theater company. It stages five big-name shows and three off-Broadway productions annually. The Rep performs in the Tennessee Performing Arts Center, located in the James K. Polk Cultural Center in downtown Nashville. This is the same building that houses the Tennessee State Museum, plus the Nashville Opera Association and the Nashville Ballet. Some of their productions have included *The Crucible, I Hate Hamlet,* and *Doubt.* The season runs from October to May.

FAMOUS NASHVILLIANS

Nashville is used to celebrity, what with all the country music stars around. But it's not just musicians who call, or called, Nashville home:

"Jefferson Street Joe" Gilliam, one of the first African-American quarterbacks in the National Football League, played his college ball at Tennessee State University. The former quarterback for the Pittsburgh Steelers died in 2000 in his hometown of Nashville, five days before his 50th birthday.

Madison Smartt Bell was born and raised in Nashville. The novelist's works include *All Souls Rising, Ten Indians,* and *The Year of Silence.*

Oprah Winfrey was raised in Nashville by her father, Vernon. In her second year at Tennessee State University she was hired as Nashville's first female and first African-American TV news anchor on WTVF-TV.

Julian Bond, civil rights activist, political activist, and the chairman of the NAACP, was born in Nashville and lived here until he was five years old.

Bobby Jones, host of BET's Bobby Jones Gospel, was once a professor at Tennessee State University. The program is the longest-running show on cable television and is taped in Nashville.

Red Grooms was born and raised in Nashville. Grooms is a prominent modern American artist, whose pop art depicts frenetic scenes of urban life.

Al Gore Jr., though born in Washington, D.C., and raised in Carthage, Tennessee, is closely associated with Nashville. After the Vietnam War he attended Vanderbilt University for one year and then spent five years as a reporter for the *Tennessean.* The former U.S. vice president and his wife, Tipper, have had a home in Nashville for many decades.

Artists' Cooperative Theatre (615/726-2281, www.act1online.com) is an organization dedicated to bringing theatrical gems, both classic and modern, to Nashville audiences. Founded in 1989, ACT 1, as it is called, has presented productions of more than 90 of the world's greatest plays. Each year the theater puts on four or five productions. ACT 1 performs at the Darkhorse Theater at 4610 Charlotte Avenue.

New theatrical works are given the spotlight by the **Actors Bridge Ensemble** (1312 Adams St., 615/341-0300, www.actorsbridge.org), a theater company for new and seasoned actors. The Ensemble brings provocative and new plays to Nashville, often performing at the Belmont Black Box Theater in midtown.

Circle Players (www.circleplayers.net) is the oldest nonprofit, all-volunteer arts association in Nashville. As a community theater, all actors, stagehands, directors, and other helpers are volunteers. The company stages four or five performances every year at a variety of theater locations around the city. Performances include classic theater, plus stage adaptations of popular cinema and literature.

Nashville's leading experimental theater group is the **People's Branch Theatre** (615/254-0008, www.peoplesbranch.org). Founded in 2000, the group brings together local actors to produce bold and innovative professional theater. They perform at the Belcourt Theatre in Hillsboro Village.

Children's Theater

Nashville Children's Theatre (724 2nd Ave. S., 615/254-9103, www.nashvillechildrenstheatre.org) is the oldest children's theater company in the United States. During the school year, the theater puts on plays for children from preschool to elementary-school age in its colorful theater. In the summer there are drama classes for youngsters.

Teenagers own and operate the **Real Life Players,** a stalwart theater company that produces original plays written by Nashville teens. Profits are donated to teen-related community organizations. Plays are performed at the

Darkhorse Theater at 4610 Charlotte Avenue. Call the theater at 615/297-7113 to find out when the next Real Life performance will be held.

Don't miss the **Marionette Shows at the Nashville Public Library** (615 Church St., 615/862-5800). Using marionettes from the collection of former library puppeteer Tom Tichenor, plus others acquired from Chicago's Peekabo Puppet Productions, the library's children's room staff put on excellent one-of-a-kind family entertainment.

Music

The **Nashville Symphony Orchestra** (One Symphony Place, 615/687-6400, www.nashvillesymphony.org) is now housed in the Schermerhorn Symphony Center next to the Country Music Hall of Fame. Nominated for four Grammies and selling more recordings than any other American orchestra, the symphony is a source of pride for Music City. Costa Rican conductor Giancarlo Guerrero will begin his tenure as music director in 2009.

The symphony puts on more than 200 performances each year, including classical, pops, and children's concerts. Its season spans September to May. Buying tickets online is a breeze, especially since you can easily choose where you want to sit. There is free parking for symphony-goers in the Sun Trust parking garage on the corner of 4th Avenue and Commerce Street.

During the summer, the symphony plays its **Centennial Park Concert Series.** Come to the Centennial Park band shell to hear free big-band, ballroom, and classical concerts.

The **Blair School of Music** (2400 Blakemore Ave., 615/322-7651) presents student, faculty, and visiting artist recitals frequently during the school year. Vanderbilt University's music school, Blair addresses music through academic, pedagogical, and performing activities.

Listen to new works by American composers performed by the **Nashville Chamber Orchestra** (615/322-1226, www.nco.org). The orchestra's concerts include masterpieces and new works commissioned by the chamber

orchestra, many of which fuse tradition with new genres, including jazz, Celtic, Latin, and world music.

Opera

Middle Tennessee's only opera association, the **Nashville Opera Association** (www.nashvilleopera.org) puts on an average of four main-stage performances per season (October–April) and does a six-week tour to area schools. They perform at the Tennessee Performing Arts Center at 505 Deaderick Street.

Ballet

Founded in 1981 as a civic dance company, the **Nashville Ballet** (www.nashvilleballet.com) became a professional dance company in 1986. Entertaining more than 40,000 patrons each year, the ballet performs both classical and contemporary pieces at the Tennessee Performing Arts Center at 505 Deaderick Street.

Dinner Theater

Chaffin's Barn Dinner Theatre (8204 Hwy. 100, 615/646-9977, www.dinnertheatre.com, $33–50) was Nashville's first professional theater and continues to put on popular Broadway-style plays for dinner patrons. If mystery is more your style, have dinner at **Miss Marple's Mystery Dinner Theatre** (135 2nd Ave. N., 615/242-8000, www.missmarples.com, $50), where you and your friends try to guess who done it.

Cinemas

Once the home of the Grand Ole Opry, the **Belcourt Theatre** (2102 Belcourt Ave., 615/383-9140, www.belcourt.org) is Nashville's best venue for independent films. Built in 1925 as a silent movie house, the Belcourt now screens a refreshing variety of independent and unusual films.

More mainstream arty flicks are shown at the **Regal Cinemas Green Hills** (3815 Green Hills Village, 615/269-5910). Mainstream multiplex cinemas can be found on the outskirts of town in nearly every direction.

FAN FAIR

Like country music itself, the annual event known as Fan Fair has evolved from a down-home meet-and-greet to large-scale musical theater.

Fan Fair began in 1972 as a convention for music fans. Each year, the event grew as more and more people wanted to meet their country idols in person. Fans bought tickets months in advance, camped out at the state fairgrounds, and yearned to see, touch, and speak with the stars. Fan Fair delivered. Stars endured marathon autograph sessions – Garth Brooks famously spent 23 hours signing autographs without a bathroom break – and they performed to crowds of their most dedicated fans.

But country music's remarkable boom of the 1990s was the end of that kind of Fan Fair – the music simply outgrew the event. Country music was no longer the step-child of the recording industry; it was corporate, and it was big business. Fans, politicians, and industry representatives tangled over the future of Fan Fair. One plan to move Fan Fair to the Nashville Superspeedway in Lebanon was nixed because it would take the event out of Nashville.

In the end, the CMA (Country Music Association) Music Festival replaced Fan Fair in 2000. With venues at Riverfront Park and LP Field, there is still plenty of music. Stars perform day and night. The autograph sessions continue in the Nashville Convention Center, but the artists you'll find here are the unknowns and up-and-comings. You need an invitation to meet and greet the stars.

The rebirth of Fan Fair as the CMA Music Festival still attracts criticism, especially from those who remember the glory days of the old Fan Fair. But today's fans delight in the modern event, and even some of the critics are coming around.

EVENTS
February

The second week of February is **Antiques Week** in Nashville. During this period, four separate antiques events top the bill. At the Tailgate Antique Show at the Fiddler's Inn Hotel in Music Valley, antiques dealers set up their shops in hotel rooms and parking spaces. A similar set-up exists at the Radisson Hotel Opryland for the Music Valley Antiques Market. The biggest sale is at the Gaylord Opryland Hotel and Convention Center. The final event for Antiques Week is the upscale Antiques and Garden Show of Nashville, which features antique dealers, exhibition gardens, and lectures at the Nashville Convention Center.

April

Nashville celebrates the coming of spring in a big way. **Awesome April** (www.visitmusiccity.com) is the name that encompasses the half dozen or more big events that take place during this month, one of the most pleasant on the city's weather calendar.

The **Country Music Television Music Awards** (www.cmt.com) was country music's first fan-voted awards show. Founded in 2002, the show lets fans participate in both the first and final rounds of voting. The show is broadcast live on television from Nashville, usually from the Curb Event Center at Belmont University.

Gospel music hosts its annual awards night in April too. The **Gospel Music Association Dove Awards** (www.gospelmusic.org) is billed as gospel music's biggest night. The celebration takes place at the Grand Ole Opry House in Music Valley, and is preceded by Gospel Music Week at the Nashville Convention Center, part trade show and part fan fair.

Film lovers throughout Tennessee look forward to the **Nashville Film Festival** (www.nashvillefilmfestival.org) held every April at the Green Hills Cinema 16. The film festival was founded in 1969 as the Sinking Creek Film Celebration. These days, upwards of 20,000 people attend the weeklong event, which includes film screenings, industry panels, and lots of parties.

Tin Pan South (www.tinpansouth.com) is an annual celebration of songs and songwriting organized by the Nashville Songwriters Association International. The event features five nights of performances by some of the best singers and songwriters around. Shows are held in 10 different intimate venues around the city, presenting music fans with the tough choice of where to go each night.

The **Country Music Marathon** (www.cm-marathon.com) takes place every April. More than 15,000 professional and amateur runners take part, and tens of thousands more come out for the live music and cheer squads that line the racecourse. The post-race concert usually boasts nationally known country music artists.

May

Held in Centennial Park, the **Tennessee Crafts Fair** (www.tennesseecrafts.org) showcases the work of more than 180 different fine craftsmen and women. More than 45,000 people come to the three-day event every year, which also includes craft demonstrations, a food fair, and entertainment. The fair repeats in September.

For something a little different, plan to attend the **Running of the Iroquois Steeplechase** (www.iroquoissteeplechase.org) at Percy Warner Park. Taking place on the second Saturday of May, the race is the nation's oldest continuously run weight-for-age steeplechase in the country. Fans in sundresses or suspenders and hats enjoy watching some of the top horses in the country navigate the race course. You can pay $15 general admission to sit on the hillside overlooking the stadium. Pack a blanket, food, and drinks, and you'll have an excellent day. Various tailgating tickets are available and are priced according to how good the view is from the parking spot. If you want to tailgate, you need to buy tickets well in advance.

Taking place every weekend in May, the **Tennessee Renaissance Festival** (www.tnrenfest.com) celebrates all things medieval. Come to watch jousting matches, hear 16th-

century comedy, or buy capes and swords. The festival takes place off Highway 96 between Franklin and Murfreesboro, about 25 minutes' drive south from Nashville.

June

What was once called Fan Fair, and is now called the **Country Music Association Music Festival** (www.cmafest.com), is a four-day music mega-show in downtown Nashville. The stage at Waterfront Park along the Cumberland River is occupied by day with some of the top names in country music. At night the hordes move to LP Field across the river to hear a different show every night. Four-day passes, which cost between $80 and $300 per person, also give you access to the exhibit hall, where you can get autographs and meet up-and-coming country music artists. This is Nashville's biggest event of the year, and you are wise to buy your tickets and book your hotel early. Get a room downtown so you don't need a car; parking and traffic is a nightmare during the festival.

Early June sees Nashville's gay, lesbian, bisexual, and transgender community show its colors at the **Nashville Pride Festival** (www.nashvillepride.org), a one-day event at Centennial Park.

July

Independence Day (www.visitmusiccity.com) is celebrated in a big way with fireworks and a riverfront concert that's broadcast live on television. The event is free and attracts upwards of 100,000 people every year.

The **Music City Brewer's Festival** (www.musiccitybrewersfest.com) is a one-day event on the lawn behind the Hilton Hotel downtown. Come to taste local brews, learn about making your own beer, and enjoy good food and live music. Tickets are required, and the event often sells out.

August

The **East Nashville Tomato Art Festival** (www.tomatoartfest.com) is a tongue-in-cheek celebration of tomatoes and the hip, artsy vibe of East Nashville. Events include a parade of tomatoes, the "Most Beautiful Tomato Pageant," biggest and smallest tomato contests, tomato toss, and Bloody Mary taste-off. The festival usually takes place on the second Saturday of August.

September

The Belle Meade Plantation (www.bellemeadeplantation.org) hosts its biggest fundraising event of the year, **Fall Fest,** every September. The two-day festival features antiques, arts and crafts, live music, and children's activities.

Nashville's annual **Greek Festival** (615/333-1047) is hosted by the Holy Trinity Greek Orthodox Church. Nashville residents flock here for homemade Greek food and entertainment, which includes dancing and tours of the historic cathedral.

The **John Merritt Classic** (www.johnmerrittclassic.com) held over Labor Day starts with fashion shows and concerts and culminates with a football contest between the Tennessee State University Tigers and another historically black collegiate football team. The annual showdown is named for legendary former TSU football coach John Ayers Merritt.

The **Music City Jazz and Blues Festival (JAMS)** (www.nbl4u.com) over Labor Day is a two-day festival featuring jazz, blues, soul, R&B, and reggae performers. It is held at Riverfront Park along the Cumberland.

October

The **Southern Festival of Books** is held during the second full weekend of October on Legislative Plaza in downtown Nashville. Featuring book readings, autograph sessions, and discussions, the festival is a must for book lovers. It has activities for children, too. The festival is organized by Humanities Tennessee (www.tn-humanities.org).

Oktoberfest (www.nashvilleoktoberfest.com) is a Nashville tradition. Held in historic Germantown north of the Bicentennial Mall, this weekend festival is enhanced by its setting in what was once Nashville's German enclave. The events include a walk-run, church services, and a street fair with German music, food, and

other entertainment. Oktoberfest usually takes place in mid-October.

Vanderbilt's Scarritt-Bennett Center hosts the **Celebration of Cultures** (www.celebrationofcultures.org) every October in Centennial Park. This international festival features food and music from around the world.

November

Beginning in November and continuing through the new year, several Nashville institutions put up special holiday decorations. Belmont University, Travellers Rest Plantation, the Hermitage, and Belle Meade all celebrate the holiday season with special decorative flair.

December

The **Music City Bowl** (www.musiccitybowl.com) pits a Southeastern Conference team against a Big Ten rival. This nationally televised football game is held at LP Field.

SHOPPING

You'll find many good reasons to shop in Nashville. Who can pass up Western wear in Music City? Fine boutiques cater to the well-heeled in tony West End. Malls in the suburbs offer upscale department stores or outlet bargains. And downtown you'll find unique art and gifts.

One of the best all-around shopping districts is **Hillsboro Village,** the commercial district that borders Vanderbilt University in midtown. Upscale clothing stores, used books, and trendy housewares are just a few of the things you'll find in this neighborhood, best explored on foot.

Music

The Texas Troubadour, Ernest Tubb, founded his famous record store on Broadway in 1947. **Ernest Tubb's Record Shop** (417 Broadway, 615/255-7503) remains an excellent source of classic and modern country music recordings, as well as DVDs, books, clothing, and souvenirs. At the back of the shop you can see the stage where Ernest Tubb's Midnite Jamboree was recorded and aired after the Grand Ole

Opry on Saturday nights. The Jamboree still airs, but it's recorded at the Texas Troubadour Theatre in Music Valley.

For new and used CDs, DVDs, and vinyl, go to **Grimey's** (1604 8th Ave. S., 615/254-4801). Here you'll find a wide selection of not just country, but rock, folk, blues, R&B, and other genres. The staff are knowledgeable and friendly.

If you want to make your own music, head to **Gruhn Guitars** (400 Broadway, 615/256-2033), a guitar shop with one of the best reputations in the music world. Founded by guitar expert George Gruhn, the shop is considered by some the best vintage guitar shop in the world. Shiny guitars, banjos, mandolins, and fiddles looks like candy hung up on the walls of the Broadway storefront that serves both up-and-coming and established Nashville musicians.

Nashville's other guitar shop is the **Gibson Bluegrass Showcase** (Opry Mills, 615/514-2233). Part retail outlet, part live music venue, the Gibson store celebrates both the instruments and the sound of bluegrass music. You can buy fiddles, mandolins, Dobros, or guitars, and they will ship all over the world.

If country music is just one of many musical interests, head to **The Great Escape** (1925 Broadway, 615/327-0646). This record and comic book shop was founded in 1977, and continues to offer a pleasing array of used CDs, records, and cassettes for music fans. The location near Vanderbilt attracts a youthful clientele.

Western Wear

No city is better endowed with places to buy Western-style wear. The best selection is found in shops along Broadway in downtown Nashville, where you'll find hats, boots, shirts, belts, jeans, and everything else you'll need to look the part. Opry Mills, the mall next to the Grand Ole Opry, also has a good selection of Western wear.

Trail West (312 Broadway, 615/251-1711) is a one-stop shop for country clothes. **Boot Country** (304 Broadway, 615/259-1691) specializes in all styles and sizes of cowboy boots.

Music-industry men and women get dressed at **flavour** (1522-B Demonbreun, 615/254-2064), a hip clothing store on Music Row. Come here for stylish denim, cowboy boots, plus casual and dressy wear for ladies and gents. This is not your daddy's boot store; this is country music chic.

The name says it all at **Manuel Exclusive Clothier** (1922 Broadway, 615/321-5444), a clothing shop where the cowboy shirts start at $750 and jackets at over $2,000.

Even without a ton of cash you can outfit yourself in some of the best Western designs at **Katy K Designs Ranch Dressing** (2407 12th Ave. S., 615/297-4242). This is the showplace of designer Katy K's unique clothing line, which has been worn by the likes of Loretta Lynn and BR549. Ranch Dressing has a well-curated selection of vintage goods, plus clothing from other designers' lines. To find the shop, look for the giant cowgirl on the facade of an otherwise nondescript office building.

Clothing

Ginette's Boutique (2420 Elliston Pl., 615/327-1440) offers the latest fashions in women's clothes, handbags, and accessories at non-runway prices.

With two locations, one in Hillsboro Village and one downtown at 305 Church Street, **Fire Finch** (615/942-5271) is known for trendy jewelry and accessories. Its downtown location also has a few home decor items as well.

A relative newcomer on the Nashville clothing scene, **Nashville Clothing Company** (2922 West End Blvd., 615/577-5346) sells stylish men's and women's clothes and shoes. This includes a wide selection of funny T-shirts, purses, and bags.

Men can get outfitted from toe to top hat at **J. Michael's Clothiers** (2525 West End Ave., 615/321-0686). An old-fashioned clothing store that specializes in one-on-one advice, J. Michael's is famous for its personal touch; in addition to selling off-the-rack name brand they tailor to suit. Whether you're just starting a new career or looking for a special-occasion outfit, you'll find what you need at J. Michael's.

Art

While not exactly a gallery, **Hatch Show Print** (316 Broadway, 615/256-2805) is one of Nashville's best-known places to buy art. Hatch has been making colorful posters for decades, and their letterpress style is now one of the trendiest looks in modern design. They continue to design and print handouts, posters, and T-shirts for local and national customers. Visitors to the shop can gaze at the cavernous warehouse operation, and buy small or large samples of their work, including reproductions of classic country music concert posters. This is a great place to find a special souvenir of your trip to Nashville.

At **All Fired Up** (21st Ave. S., 615/463-8887), choose a piece of unfinished pottery for between $5 and $50, then pay an additional $6 "painting fee," and choose from hundreds of different paints and glazes to finish your piece. This is a great way to spend a rainy afternoon or have fun with a date.

Transplanted New Yorkers Theo Antoniadis and Veta Cicolello opened **Ovvio Arte** (42 S. Chestnut St., 615/256-8756, www.ovvioarte. com) in 2008. This art gallery and performance space is a venue for the unexpected. It offers regular theater, dramatic readings, and art shows.

The Tennessee Artists Guild operates **TAG Gallery** (83 Arcade, 615/429-7708, www. tagartgallery.com), one of the best galleries in Nashville. Founded in 2000, the TAG specializes in selling affordable art to up-and-coming collectors. They offer a regular diet of unique shows.

Garage Mahal (1106 Woodland St., 615/226-2070), also known as the Art and Invention Gallery, is an East Nashville institution. Proprietors Meg and Bret MacFayden put on between five and six shows each year, including their signature Tomato Art Show, part of the annual Tomato Art Festival.

Also in East Nashville, **Plowhaus** (211 S. 17th St., 615/349-3777) is an artists' co-op with a gallery and lots of community outreach activities.

Home Decor

Find fine crystal, tableware, jewelry, and other upscale housewares at **AshBlue** (4231 Harding Rd., 615/383-4882). This sophisticated shop is perfect for bridal registries, housewarming gifts, or that special touch for your home or office.

Natural soaps, hand-crafted fragrances, and soy candles are just a few of the things you will find at **Green Pergola Aromatherapy and Soap Company** (223 Donelson Pk., 615/889-0044). One of the best things about the store, however, is its unique partnership with two other businesses. **Teas for Two** sells loose tea and **One 2 Yoga Studio** offers one-on-one and group yoga instruction. You can also buy a hot or cold cup of tea to drink while you enjoy the relaxing atmosphere of the store.

Modern home furnishings, large and small, are what draws shoppers to **Mad Mod** (162 8th Ave. N., 615/244-6807). A complete line of bamboo textiles, local art, and trendy furniture make this a popular stop for the downtown condo set.

Books

Nashville has several good bookstores, and at least one is bound to suit your taste. **Bookman Bookwoman Used Books** (1713 21st Ave. S., 615/383-6555), in the trendy Hillsboro neighborhood, is chock-a-block with used books, including cheap paperbacks and rare must-haves. **Elder's Books** (2115 Elliston Pl., 615/327-1867), close to Vanderbilt and Centennial Park, is a book-lover's bookstore. The store is packed with books, but not just any books. The collection is carefully chosen and includes many signed and first editions. Elder's has an excellent collection of books about Nashville, Tennessee, the Civil War, and the South, as well as lots of other topics. Be warned that this is a store for book-loving adults, not their children. Noisy or misbehaving children are not tolerated.

For new books, head to **Davis-Kidd Booksellers** (Green Hills Mall, 615/385-2645), a Nashville-based independent bookseller with locations throughout Tennessee. Davis-Kidd puts on a number of literary events, such as book signings, discussions, and readings.

Outloud! Books and Gifts (1701 Church St., 615/329-8006) specializes in books, videos, music, and gifts with a gay or lesbian theme. There is an adjoining café, special events, and comfortable couches for relaxing.

The newest addition to the Nashville book scene is **McKays** (5708 Charlotte Pike, 615/353-2595), which sells used books, CDs, and DVDs. A Knoxville institution for years, McKays moved to Music City in 2007. Calling itself a "free enterprise library," McKays encourages readers to return books for store credit after they've read them.

Antiques

Near 100 Oaks Mall in South Nashville you'll find Nashville's largest and most popular antiques mall. **Gaslamp Antique and Decorating Mall** (100 Powell Ave., 615/297-2224, www.gaslampantiques.com) is squeezed between a Staples and Home Depot. It has more than 150 vendors and a great selection of all types of antiques.

For something closer to town, head to **Eighth Avenue Antiques Mall** (2015 8th Ave. S., 615/279-9922) or **Wonders on Woodland** (1110 Woodland St., 615/226-5300) in East Nashville.

Malls

The finest shopping mall in Nashville is the **Mall at Green Hills,** an indoor mall located about 15 minutes' drive south from downtown Nashville along Hillsboro Road. Stores include Macy's, Dillard's, Tiffany & Co., and Davis-Kidd Booksellers. The mall has spawned additional shopping opportunities nearby, so this is a good place to head if you're in need of just about anything. Call the mall concierge (615/298-5478, ext. 22) to find out if your favorite store is there.

Farther south of Nashville, at the Moore's Lane exit off I-65, is **Cool Springs Galleria** (1800 Galleria Blvd., 615/731-6255, www. coolspringsgalleria.com), the newest mall in the area. Four major department stores

anchor the mall, which includes 100 specialty shops. The mall is surrounded by acres more of drive-up shopping centers and restaurants.

Heading west from town on Highway 70, you'll run into **Bellevue Center** (7620 U.S. 70, 615/646-8690, www.bellevuecenter.com), where you'll find Dillard's, Sears, Hecht's, and more than 115 specialty shops. Many Nashvillians consider this the city's best mall.

Outlet Malls

Some Nashville residents look down their nose at **Opry Mills** (433 Opry Mills Dr., 615/514-1000), the discount mall in Music Valley that sits across the street from the Grand Ole Opry. Indeed, if upscale shopping is your thing, don't come here. But if good deals on name-brand merchandise appeal to you, Opry Mills is the mall for you. Brands include Corning, Levi's, Banana Republic, American Eagle Outfitters, Barnes & Noble, Gap, and Off Fifth. There is also a 20-screen movie theater, IMAX, and Bass Pro Shop with all sorts of outdoor equipment.

A bit farther down the highway in Lebanon, about 30 miles east of Nashville on I-40, **Prime Outlets** (800/617-2588) features name-brand outlet stores. Brands include Polo Ralph Lauren, Coach, Tommy Hilfiger, and Ann Taylor. To get to Prime Outlets, take I-40 east from Nashville and get off at exit 238.

Flea Markets

Nashville's largest flea market takes place on the fourth weekend of every month at the Tennessee State Fairgrounds. The **Tennessee State Fairgrounds Flea Market** (615/862-5016, www.tennesseestatefair.org) is a bargain-lover's dream, with thousands of sellers peddling clothes, crafts, and all sorts of vintage and used housewares. The fairgrounds are located on 4th Avenue, south of downtown.

The **Nashville Farmer's Market** next to the Bicentennial Mall downtown has a flea market on weekends.

Sports and Recreation

Nashville has good parks, numerous sports teams, and nice weather to enjoy both.

PARKS

Centennial Park

Nashville's best city park, Centennial is best-known as home of the Parthenon. It is also a pleasant place to relax. A small lake provides a habitat for ducks and other water creatures; paved walking trails are popular for walking during nice weather. The park hosts numerous events during the year, including Shakespeare in the Park.

Radnor Lake State Natural Area

Just seven miles southwest of downtown Nashville, Radnor Lake State Natural Area (Otter Creek Rd., 615/373-3467) provides a natural escape for visitors and residents of the city. Eighty-five-acre Radnor Lake was created in 1914 by the Louisville and Nashville Railroad Company, which impounded Otter Creek to do so. The lake was to provide water for the railroad's steam engines. By the 1940s, the railroad's use of the lake ended and 20 years later the area was threatened by development. Local residents, including the Tennessee Ornithological Society, successfully rallied against development and Radnor Lake State Natural Area was established in 1973.

There are six miles of hiking trails around the lake, and Otter Creek Road, which is closed to vehicular traffic, is open to bicycles and walkers. A nature museum at the visitors center describes some of the 240 species of birds and hundreds of species of plants and animals that live at Radnor. The visitors center is open Sunday–Thursday 9 A.M.–4 P.M. and Friday–Saturday 8 A.M.–4 P.M.

Radnor is well-used and well-loved by Nashvillians, and for good reason. Very few American cities have such a large and pristine natural area so close to the urban center.

Edwin and Percy Warner Parks

The largest city parks in Tennessee, Edwin and Percy Warner Parks (Hwy. 100) are a 2,600-acre oasis of forest, fields, and quiet pathways located just nine miles southwest from downtown Nashville. Nashvillians come here to walk, jog, ride bikes and horses, and much more. The parks have scenic drives, picnic facilities, playgrounds, cross-country running trails, an equestrian center, bridle trails, a model-airplane field, and athletic fields. Percy Warner Park is also home to the Harpeth Hills Golf Course, and Edwin Percy Park has a nature center that provides year-round environmental education. The nature center also hands out maps and other information about the park.

Warner Parks hosts the annual Iroquois Steeplechase Horse Race in May. A 10-mile bridle path is open to horseback riding year-round. Visit the park's Equestrian Center (2500 Old Hickory Blvd.) for more information.

J. Percy Priest Lake

J. Percy Priest Lake was created in the mid-1960s when the Army Corps of Engineers dammed Stones River east of Nashville. The lake is a favorite destination for fishing, boating, swimming, and picnicking.

J. Percy Priest Lake sprawls over 14,200 acres. Access is provided through more than a dozen different parks and access areas on all sides of the lake. Many of these areas bear the names of communities that were inundated when the lake was created.

The lake's main visitors center, operated by the Army Corps of Engineers, is located at the site of the dam that created the lake. The visitors center is located on Bell Road at exit 219 off I-40 heading east from downtown Nashville. There you will find a lake overlook and one of four marinas on the lake.

In addition to access areas managed by the Corps of Engineers, Nashville operates **Hamilton Creek Park** on the western shore of the lake. The State of Tennessee operates **Long Hunter State Park** on the eastern shore.

There are several hiking trails around the lake. The **Three Hickories Nature Trail** is an easy 1.6-mile trail found in the Cook Recreational Area. **Anderson Road Fitness Trail** is a paved one-mile trail that travels through woodlands and along the lake.

For a long hike, or for horseback riding, go to the **Twin Forks Horse Trail,** an 18-mile trail located in the East Fork Recreation Area on the southwestern shore of the lake. Within Long Hunter State Park there are three hiking trails, including a nature loop trail and the mile-long Deer Trail leaving from the visitors center.

Boating, fishing, and watersports are among the most popular activities on J. Percy Priest Lake. Launch ramps are found in Long Hunter State Park and at several marinas around the lake. Elm Hill Marina (3361 Bell Rd., 615/889-5363, www.elmhillmarina.com) is the marina closest to downtown Nashville.

The Corps of Engineers operates three day-use swim areas that have sand beaches, bathrooms, and other amenities for a day in the water. These swim areas are located at Anderson Road, Cook Campground, and Seven Points Campground. There is a $4 per-vehicle fee at Anderson and Cook. There is swimming at Long Hunter State Park's Bryant Grove as well.

GOLF

Nashville operates seven public golf courses in the city. Many of these are in parks and offer excellent golf in beautiful settings. You can find details about all city courses at www.nashville.gov/parks/golf/golf.htm. Most courses are open year-round; call ahead for operating hours and to reserve a tee time.

Harpeth Hills Golf Course (2424 Old Hickory Blvd., 615/862-8493) is a par-72 course built in 1965 and renovated in 1991. It is located in Percy Warner Park, and is considered one of Tennessee's best public golf courses. Green fees are $23 on weekdays and $25 on weekends.

Percy Warner Park is home of **Percy Warner Golf Course,** a nine-hole course good for beginner golfers, available on a walk-in basis only.

Probably the most-used public golf course in Nashville, **McCabe Golf Course** (615/862-8491) is located in West Nashville near Sylvan Park. McCabe consists of a par-70 18-hole course and 9-hole course. Upgrades have introduced new green complexes and tee complexes. Green fees are $20 on weekdays and $22 on weekends.

The oldest city golf course in Nashville is **Shelby Golf Course** (615/862-8474), located in Shelby Park in East Nashville. Shelby is a short course with small mounded greens that places a premium on accuracy. Green fees are $16.

Situated on the Cumberland River in North Nashville, **Ted Rhodes Golf Course** (615/862-8463) is scenic, and pleasant to walk. Built in 1953 as a nine-hole course, Ted Rhodes was expanded to 18 holes in 1992. It is par 72. Green fees are $20 on weekdays and $22 on weekends.

Located near Music Valley in Donelson, **Two Rivers Golf Course** (615/889-2675) offers a challenging course for golfers of all skill levels. A bonus is the view of the Nashville skyline at the eighth hole. Greens fees are $20 on weekdays and $22 on weekends.

There are many privately owned golf courses in Nashville, some of which are open to the public. **Gaylord Springs** (18 Springhouse Ln., 615/458-1730), located next to the Gaylord Opryland Hotel in Music Valley, is a par-72 18-hole course built in 1990. Greens fees are $50–90. **Nashboro Golf Club** (1101 Nashboro Blvd., 615/367-2311) offers a par-72 18-hole course with fees between $27 and $41. **Hillwood Country Club** (6201 Hickory Valley Rd., 615/352-5600) is a par-72 6,903-yard course built in 1955. Greens fees are around $85.

BIKING

The first destination for bikers around Nashville is the **Natchez Trace Parkway** (www.nps.gov/natr), a two-lane 444-mile blacktop scenic drive that originates in Nashville and journeys south through Tennessee and Mississippi countryside, eventually terminating in Natchez, Mississippi. The parkway is closed to commercial traffic and the speed limit is strictly enforced, making it popular for biking.

Biking the Trace can be an afternoon outing or a weeklong adventure. The National Park Service maintains three campgrounds along the Trace, plus five bicyclist-only campsites with more modest amenities. The northernmost bike campsite is located at the intersection of the Trace and Highway 50, about 36 miles south of Nashville.

When biking on the Trace, ride in a single-file line and always wear reflective clothing and a helmet. Pack food and water, and carry a cell phone, ID, and emergency information.

Short paved trails good for biking can be found at Radnor Lake State Natural Area, Warner Parks, and in any of Nashville's greenways, including those at Shelby Bottoms along the Cumberland River.

Nashville's only dedicated mountain bike trail is at **Hamilton Creek Park** (www.hamcreek.com) on J. Percy Priest Lake, on the east side of the Nashville airport. This 10-mile bike trail consists of an eastern trail better for beginning bikers and a western trail for advanced bikers. The two trails meet at a tunnel that crosses Bell Road.

Bike Shops

There are several good bike shops in Nashville. If you need bike gear, repairs, or advice, check out **Cumberland Transport** (2807 West End Ave., 615/321-4069), **Nashville Bicycle Company** (2817 West End Ave., 615/321-5510), or **Trace Bikes** (8400 Hwy. 100, 615/646-2485), located next to the Loveless Café near the Natchez Trace Parkway.

Resources

If you're looking for the inside scoop on biking around Nashville and recommended routes in the surrounding countryside, check out www.nashvillecyclist.com, an online community of bikers.

The **Harpeth Bike Club** (www.

harpethbikeclub.com) is Nashville's largest bike club. It organizes weekend and weekday group rides from April to October, plus races and social events where you can meet other bike enthusiasts.

TENNIS

The **Centennial Sportsplex** (222 25th Ave. N., 615/862-8480, www.sportsplextennis.com) has 15 lighted outdoor tennis courts and four indoor courts, as well as a ball machine, pro shop, and concession stand. The center is open seven days a week; specific hours vary by season. Indoor court rental fees are $18 per hour; courts may be booked up to three days in advance. Outdoor courts are available for $3 per hour per person and they can be reserved up to six days in advance.

The Sportsplex organizes numerous tennis tournaments, leagues, and classes during the year. Call or stop by for details.

SWIMMING

The city's biggest pool is found at the **Centennial Sportsplex Aquatic Center** (222 25th Ave. N., 615/862-8480, www.centennialsportsplex.com, Mon.–Thurs. 5:30 A.M.–7:50 P.M., Fri. 5:30 A.M.–5:50 P.M., Sat. 9 A.M.–4:50 P.M., adults $6, children under 13, military, disabled, seniors, and students $5, children 4 and under free). The center, located near Centennial Park in midtown, has both a large lap pool and a small play pool. Various swim classes are offered; call for a schedule.

Take the kids to **Wave Country** (2320 Two Rivers Pkwy., 615/885-1052, daily 10 A.M.–6 P.M., adults $8, children under 12 $7, children under 4 free), a waterpark with exciting slides, wave pool, and sand volleyball courts. Wave Country is managed by the city parks commission, and is open from Memorial Day to Labor Day.

A great destination for swimming and watersports is **Nashville Shores** (4001 Bell Rd., Hermitage, 615/889-7050, www.nashvilleshores.com, Mon–Sat. 10 A.M.–6 P.M., Sun. 11 A.M.–6 P.M.). Here you'll find miles of sandy beaches along the shore of J. Percy

Priest Lake, pools, waterslides, and watersports. Admission includes the opportunity to take a 45-minute lake cruise. Admission rates are based on height; 48 inches and taller pay $22, shorter than that $17. Children two years and under are free. General admission is half-price after 3 P.M. Nashville Shores is open from Memorial Day to Labor Day.

GYMS

The City of Nashville operates a fitness center in the **Centennial Sportsplex** (222 25th Ave. N., 615/862-8480, www.centennialsportsplex.com, Mon.–Thurs. 5:30 A.M.–8 P.M., Fri. 5:30 A.M.–6 P.M., Sat. 9 A.M.–5 P.M., adults $6, children under 13, military, disabled, seniors, and students $5, children 4 and under free). The fitness center has modern cardiovascular and weight-lifting machines. Fitness classes are also offered.

The Sportsplex also has two pools, tennis courts, and an ice rink. The ice rink offers public skate periods every week, with more during the winter months and holiday season.

SPECTATOR SPORTS
Football
You simply cannot miss 68,000-seat LP Field, home of the **Tennessee Titans** (460 Great Circle Rd., 615/565-4000, www.titansonline.com). The stadium, which was finished in 1999, towers on the east bank of the Cumberland River, directly opposite downtown. Since their move to the stadium in 1999, the Titans have sold out each and every home game. They play from September to December.

Tickets sell out early—often months in advance. If you want to see a game on short notice, your best bet is a program where season ticket–holders can sell their seats to games they don't want to attend.

For an altogether different football experience, catch a home game of the **Nashville Dream** (615/907-6617, www.nashville-dream.com) at Glencliff High School. The Nashville Dream is a women's football team and a member of the National Women's Football Association. The season runs from April to July.

Finally, the most unique brand of football played in Nashville is Australian rules. The **Nashville Kangaroos** (www.nashvillekangaroos.org) were founded in 1997 and were one of the first Australian football teams in the United States. The "Roos" play at Elmington Park (3500 West End Ave.), and sometimes practice with Vanderbilt's own Aussie rules squad. One of the missions of the club is to promote cultural understanding and exchange, so the social calendar can be just as grueling as the sports one. The Roos also sponsor a women's netball team.

Racing
The **Nashville Superspeedway** (4847-F McGreary Rd., Lebanon, 615/547-7223, www.nashvillesuperspeedway.com) is a 1.33-mile course that hosts Indy Racing League, NASCAR Craftsman Trucks, and two NASCAR Busch Series races. Seating up to 150,000 fans, Nashville Superspeedway has been drawing capacity crowds since it opened in 2001. The Superspeedway is located in Lebanon, Tennessee, about 30 minutes' drive east of town.

Baseball
What a fine name for a minor-league baseball team! The **Nashville Sounds** (534 Chestnut St., 615/242-4371, www.nashvillesounds.com) are a AAA affiliate of the Milwaukee Brewers, and they play about 30 home games a year from June to October. Before the 2008 season opener, the team invested $1 million in stop-gap improvements to the aging Greer Stadium, their home in south Nashville. The remedial works were intended to keep the stadium running only for the next few years, and Sounds officials have said that they will need a new stadium soon.

Tickets are $10 for reserved seats or $6 general admission.

Soccer
Nashville's professional soccer team, the

Metros (Ezell Park, 5135 Harding Pl., 615/832-5678, www.nashvillemetrosoccer.com), play just south of Nashville International Airport. Founded in 1989, the Metros have endured a half-dozen name, field, and league changes. They have survived thanks to the dogged support of soccer fans in the city.

The Metros are a member of the United Soccer League's Premier Development League, and the season runs from May to July. They play other teams from the southeastern United States. Single-game tickets are $7 for adults and $4 for youths.

Ice Hockey

Nashville celebrated the 10th anniversary of its National Hockey League franchise, the **Predators** (501 Broadway, http://predators.nhl.com), in 2008. It was a sweet victory for fans, who fought to keep the team in the city in the face of lackluster support from the community. The Predators play in the 20,000-seat Sommet Center, also called the Nashville Arena, located on Broadway in the heart of downtown. The regular season begins in October and ends in early April. Single-game tickets start at $17 and can cost as much as $150.

College Sports

In addition to Nashville's smorgasbord of professional and semi-professional sports teams, the city's colleges provide lots of good spectator sports. Vanderbilt plays football, men's and women's basketball, and baseball in the Southeastern Conference. Tennessee State University and Belmont University play Division 1-A basketball, and Lipscomb University is a member of the Atlantic Sun Division.

Accommodations

Nashville has more than 32,000 hotel rooms. Accommodations range from historic downtown hotels to standard motels. Some of the city's most distinctive accommodations are in bed-and-breakfast inns in Hillsboro and East Nashville.

Downtown has the most appealing and convenient hotels. More budget-friendly options are found in midtown and Music Valley.

BROADWAY AND THE DISTRICT

Hotels in this neighborhood are as close as you can get to attractions including the Country Music Hall of Fame and Broadway honky-tonks.

$150-200

Located across Broadway from the Frist Center for the Visual Arts, **Holiday Inn Express Nashville-Downtown** (902 Broadway, 615/244-0150, $150) offers a comfortable compromise between value and location. There is an on-site fitness room, free wireless Internet, a business center, and a guest laundry. Guest rooms have desks, coffeemakers, and two telephones. Suites ($250) have refrigerators and microwave ovens. All guests enjoy free continental breakfast. On-site parking is available for $14 a day. The Holiday Inn is located about five blocks away from lower Broadway.

Over $200

Nashville's most notable downtown hotel is ◖ **Union Station** (1001 Broadway, 615/726-1001, $160–270), a 125-room Wyndham Hotel located in what was once the city's main train station. Distinctions include magnificent iron work and molding, and an impressive marble-floored great hall that greets guests. High ceilings and lofty interior balconies make this one of Nashville's great old buildings, and hotel guests get to make it their home away from home. Union Station is a fine hotel, with amenities like free turn-down service, a fitness center, wireless Internet, plasma televisions, complimentary morning newspapers, and room service. Rooms have cathedral ceilings, stylish furnishings, and a subtle art deco touch. The bathrooms have soaking tubs, walk-in showers, and expansive marble vanities. You can choose from a standard room with one double bed or a premium room with a king-sized bed or two double beds. Four suites are also available.

The all-suite **《 Hilton Nashville Downtown** (121 4th Ave. S., 615/620-1000, www.nashvillehilton.com, $170–240) is next door to the Country Music Hall of Fame, Broadway's honky-tonks, and the home of the Nashville Symphony. It's also across the street from the Nashville Convention Center. All of the hotel's 330 suites have two distinct rooms—a living room with sofa, cable television, microwave oven, refrigerator, and coffeemaker, and a bedroom with one or two beds. The rooms are appointed with modern, stylish furniture and amenities. An indoor pool, workout room, valet parking, and two award-winning restaurants round out the hotel's amenities. The Hilton's combination of luxury and location make it one of the best choices for travelers to Nashville.

The **Renaissance Hotel** (611 Commerce St., 615/255-8400, $290–310) is connected to the Nashville Convention Center by a raised and covered walkway. Located one block north of Broadway, it stands 25 stories, providing impressive views of the city below. The Renaissance's 646 rooms offer web TV, hairdryers and ironing boards, crisp linens, coffeemakers, and business services. For an additional $12 daily, guests can enjoy high-speed wired Internet access and unlimited local and U.S. long-distance calls. The fitness center is next door to an indoor heated swimming pool, whirlpool, and sauna.

DOWNTOWN

Downtown hotels are convenient to downtown businesses and government offices, and a short walk from tourist attractions along Broadway.

Over $200

The last of a dying breed of downtown hotels, the **《 Hermitage Hotel** (231 6th Ave., 615/244-3121, www.thehermitagehotel.com,

$300–800) has been the first choice for travelers to downtown Nashville for almost 100 years. The 123-room hotel was commissioned by prominent Nashville citizens and opened for business in 1910, quickly becoming the favorite gathering place for the city's elite. Prominent figures including Al Capone, Gene Autry, and seven U.S. presidents have stayed at the Hermitage. In modern times, its roll call includes some of country music's biggest names. You don't have to be famous to stay at the Hermitage, but having plenty of cash will help your cause. Rooms start at $300 a night, but check for last-minute specials on its website when rates will dip to $200. Guests enjoy top-of-the-line amenities, including 24-hour room service, pet walking, valet parking, and laundry services. Rooms are furnished in an opulent style befitting a luxury urban hotel, and have CD/DVD players, refreshment centers, marble baths, and high-speed wireless Internet access. Many rooms have lovely views of the Capitol and city.

Courtyard by Marriot (179 4th Ave. N., 615/256-0900, $200–250) is a 181-room renovated hotel set in a century-old downtown high-rise. It is located right next to Printer's Alley, and is set midway between the downtown business district and Broadway's entertainment attractions. Guest rooms are tastefully decorated, with web TV, wired Internet access, coffeemakers, ironing boards, cable TV, voice mail, and super-comfortable beds. There are two restaurants on-site, and guests can take advantage of valet parking for $20 a day.

Located just steps from the Tennessee State Capitol and near dozens of downtown office buildings, the **Doubletree Hotel Nashville** (315 4th Ave. N., 615/244-8200, $190–250) is a popular choice for business travelers. Rooms are spacious and bright, and even basic rooms have a comfortable desk and chair, coffeemaker, free Internet access, voice mail, and ironing boards. The hotel boasts a beautiful indoor swimming pool, business center, above-average fitness center, and on-site restaurant and coffee shop. Parking at the Doubletree is valet only and costs $20 per day.

The **Sheraton Downtown Nashville** (623 Union St., 615/259-2000, $200–270) is a city landmark. The 476-room hotel stands tall above neighboring buildings, providing most guest rooms with views of the city below. Located in the middle of Nashville's bustling downtown business district, it is another good option for business travelers. The hotel is 100 percent smoke-free, and has a fitness room, business center, indoor pool, and laundry and concierge services. Internet access and on-site parking is available for an additional fee.

MIDTOWN
Midtown hotels are near Music Row, Vanderbilt and Belmont Universities, and the entertainment, dining, and shopping attractions of Hillsboro Village.

Under $100
One of two hostels in Nashville, **Music City Hostel** (1809 Patterson St., 615/692-1277, www.musiccityhostel.com, $25) is located among doctor's offices and commercial buildings in between downtown Nashville and Elliston Place. The low-slung '70s-style building looks like nothing much on the outside, but inside it is cheerful, welcoming, and a comfortable home base for budget travelers. Music City Hostel offers the usual dorm-style bunk-bed accommodations, as well as a handful of private apartments, which rent for $75–85 a night. You can also have a private bedroom with private bath plus shared kitchen and common room for $60 a night. Common areas include a large kitchen, dining room, reading room, cable TV room, computer with Internet access, and a coin laundry. The entire facility is smoke-free. Parking is free, and the hostel is within walking distance of restaurants, a bus stop, car rental agency, post office, and hospitals. It would be a hike to get downtown on foot from here.

$100-150
Best Western Music Row (1407 Division St., 615/242-1631, $90–110) is a no-nonsense motel with an outdoor pool, free continental breakfast, Internet access, and indoor corridors. Rooms have cable TV, AM/FM alarm clocks, and coffeemakers. Pets are allowed for $10 a day, and parking is free. The 75-room hotel is located a few steps away from the Music Row traffic circle and nearby restaurants.

Located near Elliston Place and Vanderbilt University, **Guesthouse Inn and Suites** (1909 Hayes St., 615/329-1000, $109) offers a free shuttle to nearby hospitals, including Baptist Hospital, Vanderbilt Medical Center, and the Veterans Administration Hospital. All rooms have microwave ovens, refrigerators, and coffeemakers, and guests enjoy free breakfast including made-to-order waffles. Suites ($140) include a sleeper couch. Rooms are typical motel-style, with two double beds or a single king-sized bed. The property is convenient to Hillsboro Village, Music Row, and Centennial Park.

Come home to **Hillsboro House** (1933 20th Ave. S., 615/292-5501, www.visitnashville.net, $130–175), a restored Victorian buttercup cottage in a quiet residential neighborhood near Vanderbilt, Hillsboro Village, and Belmont University. The bed-and-breakfast offers three mini-suites, each with a private bathroom and telephone. Rooms have comfortable feather beds, antique furniture, and touches of home. Guests are invited to lounge in an upstairs library. There is free wireless Internet access for guests, and the full breakfast includes homemade breads.

Another bed-and-breakfast choice in this part of the city is **1501 Linden House Bed and Breakfast** (1501 Linden Ave., 615/298-2701, www.nashville-bed-breakfast.com, $110–165). This cheerful yellow-brick home on a corner lot has three guest rooms, each with stylish furniture and hardwood floors; one room has a private whirlpool and another has a fireplace.

Over $200
For luxurious accommodations near Vanderbilt, choose ❰ **Loews Vanderbilt Plaza** (2100 West End Ave., 615/320-1700, $260–310), a 340-room hotel on West End Avenue close to Centennial Park and Hillsboro Village. Loews

boasts 24-hour room service, luxurious sheets, towels, and robes, natural soaps, and spacious bathrooms. Guests enjoy top-of-the-line coffee and tea kettles, evening turn-down service, and free high-speed Internet access. Many rooms have views of the Nashville skyline; premium rooms provide guests with access to the concierge lounge, with continental breakfast and evening hors d'oeuvres and a cash bar. All guests can enjoy a fine fitness room, spa, art gallery, and gift shop.

You can't get closer to Vanderbilt University than the **Marriott Nashville Vanderbilt** (2555 West End Ave., 615/321-1300, $180–300). Set on the northern end of the university campus, the Marriott has 301 guest rooms, six suites, and meeting space. It is located across West End Avenue from Centennial Park, home of the Parthenon, and a few steps from Vanderbilt's football stadium. There is an indoor pool, full-service restaurant, deli, concierge lounge, ATM, and business center.

EAST NASHVILLE

While it does not have many attractions, there are a few good reasons to stay in East Nashville. For football fans, this part of the city is close to the Tennessee Titans' stadium. Others will enjoy bed-and-breakfasts in Edgefield, a cool, laid-back, and diverse residential neighborhood. Good dining abounds, and downtown is a short drive or walk across the Cumberland River.

Under $100

Located on the east bank of the Cumberland River, **Days Inn at the Stadium** (211 N. 1st St., 615/254-1551, $75–100) is near LP Field, where the Tennessee Titans play. The hotel's 180 rooms have clock-radios, cable TV, and wireless Internet. Some have nice views of the Nashville skyline. Guests enjoy access to a fitness room, indoor pool, and laundry facilities, plus free breakfast. There is a bar and restaurant inside the hotel. While not within easy walking distance of downtown Nashville, the Days Inn is just across the river from the city's premier attractions. Free parking is a plus.

$100-150

Carole's Yellow Cottage (801 Fatherland St., 615/226-2952, $100–125) is a bed-and-breakfast offering two comfortable guest rooms. The decor is not as fussy as many bed-and-breakfasts, and the atmosphere is homey and low-key. Rooms have a private bathroom, and guests can relax in a library with a TV/VCR. Breakfasts are homemade and feature organic foods when available.

The Big Bungalow (618 Fatherland St., 615/256-8375, www.thebigbungalow.com, $110–160), a Craftsman-style early-1900s townhouse, offers three guest rooms, each with its own private bath and television. Guests have shared access to a computer, microwave, and refrigerator. Common areas are comfortable and stylish, with tasteful decor and hardwood floors. Hostess Ellen Warshaw prepares breakfast for her guests and sometimes hosts in-the-round concerts in her living room. She is also a licensed masseuse. This is a pet-free, non-smoking facility; children over 10 years are welcome. The bed-and-breakfast is located about seven blocks from the Shelby Street Pedestrian Bridge that takes you to the heart of the District.

$150-200

The East Park Inn (822 Boscoble St., 615/226-8691, $155) is a brightly painted Queen Anne–style bed-and-breakfast in Edgefield, on the east bank of the Cumberland River. Two guest suites offer private bathrooms and elegant furnishings. Guests also enjoy a relaxing terrace and garden, comfortable common rooms, and delicious breakfasts of fresh fruit, breads, quiche, waffles, and fresh-squeezed orange juice, served by host Brooks Parker. Afternoon tea or wine is served on the front porch, which enjoys a pleasant view of the Nashville skyline. The inn is located 10 blocks from downtown Nashville, and three blocks from coffee shops and restaurants.

You'll be happy to call **Top O' Woodland** (1603 Woodland St., 888/288-368, www.topofwoodland.com, $160) home during your stay in Nashville. This redbrick home on a corner lot is distinctive and beautiful. Features include a spacious wraparound front porch, original stained-glass windows, a turret, a baby grand Steinway piano, and lots of period and original antiques. The bed-and-breakfast is within five blocks of restaurants and pubs, and a short drive over the Cumberland to downtown Nashville. Guests can choose to stay in the master suite, with a king-sized four-poster bed, working fireplace, private bath, and private entrance, or in Mr. Green's Cottage, a detached cottage with kitchenette that can sleep up to six people. The home has wireless high-speed Internet access, and a generous continental breakfast is served at your convenience. Hostess Belinda Leslie is a chaplain and a certified wedding and event planner, and Top O'Woodland is a beautiful place for an old-fashioned wedding or quiet elopement.

MUSIC VALLEY

There are a dozen or more chain hotels in Music Valley, all close to restaurants and a short drive from the Grand Ole Opry and Opry Mills mall. Nashville's most famous hotel, Opryland, is luxurious and within walking distance of the Opry.

These hotels tend to provide more for your money than downtown digs, but they are a 10-to-15-minute drive to the city center.

Under $100

If you're looking for a clean, comfortable room and friendly welcome, look no farther than the **(Fiddler's Inn** (2410 Music Valley Dr., 615/885-1440, www.fiddlers-inn.com, $60–75). This 204-room no-frills hotel offers a solid Tennessee welcome to its guests, who come in droves to see the Opry and enjoy other Music Valley attractions. It's right next to a Cracker Barrel restaurant and there's plenty of parking for cars and tour buses. Guests enjoy cable TV, free coffee and pastries in the morning, an outdoor pool, and a gift shop stocked with Nashville souvenirs.

The all-suite **Best Western Suites near Opryland** (201 Music City Cir., 615/902-9940, $70–80) is a comfortable compromise between the luxury of the Opryland Hotel and the affordability of a motel. Each of the hotel's 100 suites has a couch, desk, high-speed Internet access, coffee- and tea-maker, microwave, ironing board, and refrigerator. Rooms with whirlpools tubs are available for about $80 more per night. Guests enjoy an on-site fitness room, 24-hour business center, outdoor pool, free continental breakfast, and weekday newspaper. The Best Western is located along a strip of motels and restaurants about one mile from the Grand Ole Opry and other Opryland attractions.

Located about two miles from the Opryland, **Comfort Inn Opryland Area** (2516 Music Valley Dr., 615/889-0086, $70–75) offers 121 clean, comfortable guest rooms with cable TV, wireless Internet, ironing board, hair dryer, and free daily newspaper. There is free outdoor parking, and interior corridors.

$100–150

Guests at the **Courtyard by Marriott Opryland** (125 Music City Cir., 615/882-9133, $140–150) enjoy refurbished rooms with soft beds, wireless Internet, coffeemakers, ironing boards, and refrigerators. The on-site restaurant serves breakfast, and business rooms come with a desk, dataport, voice mail, and speakerphone.

Over $200

The **Gaylord Opryland Hotel** (2800 Opryland Dr., 615/889-1000, $240–310) feels like a cruise ship on land. This 2,881-room luxury hotel and convention center is built around a nine-acre indoor garden. Glass atriums invite sunlight, and miles of footpaths invite you to explore the climate-controlled gardens. Highlights include a 40-foot waterfall and flatboats that float along a river.

Set among the gardens are dozens of different restaurants and cafés, ranging from casual buffets to elegant steakhouses. A few shops are sprinkled in, but it has not yet totally morphed into a mall. Hundreds of room balconies overlook the gardens, providing some guests with views of the well-kept greenery, even in winter. If you stay, choose between a "traditional view" looking outside the hotel, or an "atrium view" for about $60 more per night.

The property has a full-service salon and fitness center, on-site child care and "kid's resort," and a car rental agency. You can walk to Opry Mills mall and the Grand Ole Opry from the hotel or take the free shuttle. Guest rooms are luxurious and feature coffee- and tea-makers; two telephones; wireless Internet access; pay-per-view movies, games, and music; daily national newspapers; and other usual amenities. You can add a refrigerator for a one-time $20 fee, and you get up to 20 minutes of local calls free per day. Guests can buy one-time or daily passes on the downtown shuttle for about $15 a day, and the airport shuttle costs $35 round-trip.

While room rates at the Opryland are steep, the hotel offers attractive packages that add on other Gaylord-owned attractions and properties. These often include tickets to the Grand Ole Opry, a ride on the General Jackson Showboat, trips into Nashville to visit the Ryman Auditorium or the Wildhorse Saloon, and extras like spa visits and golf games at the hotel. Many of these packages are a good deal for travelers who want to pay one price for their whole vacation.

AIRPORT
Under $100

The **Alexis Inn and Suites Nashville Airport** (600 Ermac Dr., 615/889-4466, www.nash-villealexishotel.com, $60–70) is a comfortable and convenient place to stay near the airport. Rooms have all the usual amenities, plus guests get free popcorn in the lobby, a free airport shuttle daily between 7 A.M. and 9 P.M., and a business center. All rooms have refrigerators, and most have microwaves. There is a free continental breakfast. Suites cost $80–100 per night.

$100-150

Drury Inns and Suites (555 Donelson Pike, 615/902-0400, $100–130) offers guests an appealing array of extras, including a free hot breakfast, free evening beverages and snacks, a free airport shuttle, 60 minutes of free long-distance calls, and $7 daily park-and-fly parking. There is both an indoor and outdoor pool and a fitness center. Drury Inn is about two miles north of the airport and five miles south of Music Valley.

Hotel Preston (733 Briley Pkwy., 615/361-5900, www.hotelpreston.com, $110–140) is a boutique hotel near the airport. Youthful energy, modern decor, and up-to-date rooms set this property apart from the crowd. Rooms are stocked with Tazo tea and Starbucks coffee and there's an a 24-hour fitness center. The "You-Want-It-You-Got-It" button in each room beckons the 24-hour room service, and whimsical extras including a lava lamp, pet fish, and art kit are available by request when you check in. High-speed Internet is an add-on extra. Naughty packages—like the "Ooey Gooey Night Out" couple's getaway with late checkout, wine, and whipped cream on request—prove that this isn't your parents' motel, though the hotel caters equally to business travelers with meeting rooms and a business center. Two restaurants, including a bar and nightclub, provide food and entertainment.

SOUTH OF NASHVILLE
Under $100

Nashville's second hostel is located a half-hour drive south of the city in Brentwood. **Country Hostel Nashville** (9900 Maxwell Ln., 615/578-7207, www.countryhostelnash-ville.com, $22) is indeed semi-rural, and guests can enjoy bike riding (the hostel rents bikes) or sitting out on the comfortable deck. The hostel has free wireless Internet, a barbecue, and a spacious kitchen. It is non-smoking inside and air-conditioned in summer. Accommodations are divided into male and female dorm-style rooms with bunk beds and clean sheets. Towels and linens are provided, and the hostel will pick you up from the airport or bus station for an additional fee.

This hostel is also convenient to attractions in Franklin, Tennessee, and close to malls, shopping, and dining. You need a car to explore any of these areas, however.

NASHVILLE

Food

You can eat in a different restaurant each day in Nashville and never get bored. Southern cooking stars at meat-and-three diners and barbecue joints, fine dining restaurants cater to the well-heeled, and ethnic eateries reflect the city's diversity.

The Arcade

One of two downtown food destinations, the Arcade is an old outdoor shopping mall that lies between 4th and 5th Avenues. The ground floor of the Arcade is full of hole-in-the-wall restaurants that cater to the downtown lunchtime crowd with quick, cheap eats. Upstairs are professional offices and a few galleries.

Katie's Meat & Three (10 Arcade, 615/256-1055) has four different meat specials daily, which you can get with sides like turnip greens, mashed potatoes, and white beans. A meat-and-three plate costs $7; order your choice of four sides for $5. **The Greek Touch** (13 Arcade, 615/259-9493) has gyro, sausage, veggie, and chicken divine sandwiches, platters, and salads, all for under $6. There are also several sandwich shops, a pizza parlor, and a Chinese restaurant.

Most restaurants at the Arcade have some seating inside, or you can sit outside and watch the world go by around you. The outdoor experience is made slightly less enjoyable by the presence of smokers who have been forbidden to enter many eateries.

Nashville Farmer's Market

Organizers of the Nashville Farmer's Market have hit upon a good thing. The outdoor components of the market include a farm shed with fresh produce year-round and a flea market with arts and crafts on weekends. The interior of the market is a food court with choices ranging from Southern specialties to Caribbean cuisine. **Swett's** (900 8th Ave. N., 615/742-9699), a popular soul food restaurant, has an outpost here. **Jamaicaway** (900 8th Ave. N., 615/255-5920) serves oxtail, steamed fish, and Jamaican patties. There are also Mexican, Chinese, and

Greek choices, as well as a super salad bar. The food court is open daily 9 A.M.–5 P.M.

DINERS AND COFFEE SHOPS
Downtown

Provence (601 Church St., 615/664-1150, Mon.–Fri. 7 A.M.–6 P.M., Sat. 8 A.M.–5 P.M., $5–12), located inside the Nashville Public Library, serves excellent European-style pastries, breads, and salads, as well as coffee. Provence's signature sandwiches include creamy chicken salad and turkey-and-brie. Or you can try a sampler of the café's salads, including roasted-vegetable salad, parmesan potato salad, or creamy penne pasta. Save room for a decadent pastry, or at least a cookie, which come in varieties like raspberry hazelnut, chocolate espresso, and ginger molasses. For breakfast, nothing beats a buttery croissant spread with jam. Provence also has locations at 1600 Division Street at Roundabout Plaza; at 315 Deaderick Street in the AmSouth Building downtown; and in Hillsboro at 1705 21st Avenue South.

For homemade salads, wraps, and sandwiches, follow the crowds of downtown office workers to the **Frist Center Cafe** (919 Broadway, 616/244-3340, Mon.–Wed. and Sat. 10 A.M.–5:30 P.M., Thurs.–Fri. 10 A.M.–9 P.M., Sun. noon–5 P.M., $5–8), located at the rear of the Frist Center for the Arts. Sandwiches are available whole or half, and you can add a soup, salad, or fries for a well-rounded lunch. The café has daily hot lunch entrées, plus a case of tempting desserts.

Midtown

When Nashvillians are in the mood for a hearty deli sandwich, they head to **Noshville** (1918 Broadway, 615/329-6674, Mon. 6:30 A.M.–2:30 P.M., Tues.–Thurs. 6:30 A.M.–9 P.M., Fri. 6:30 A.M.–10:30 P.M., Sat. 7:30 A.M.–10:30 P.M., Sun. 7:30 A.M.–9 P.M., $7–12), which is as close to a genuine New York delicatessen as you'll find in this town. Lox and bagels, oatmeal, and a variety of egg dishes are popular at breakfast.

At lunch and supper choose from a variety of sandwiches, all served double-stacked, which means it's really more than any one person should eat. To find Noshville, look for the miniature statue of Lady Liberty on the roof. There is a second location in Green Hills at 4014 Hillsboro Circle, 615/269-3535.

The hype surrounding Nashville's favorite breakfast restaurant, the **Pancake Pantry** (1796 21st Ave. S., 615/383-9333, Mon.–Fri. 6 A.M.–3 P.M., Sat.–Sun. 6 A.M.–4 P.M., $6–14) is deserved. Founded in 1961 and still family-owned, the Pantry serves the best pancakes in the city, and probably the state. Owner David Baldwin says that the secret is in the ingredients, which are fresh and homemade. Many of the flours come from Tennessee, and the syrup is made right at the restaurant. The Pantry proves that a pancake can be much more than plain. The menu offers no less than 21 varieties, and that doesn't include the waffles. Try the fluffy buckwheat cakes, savory cornmeal cakes, sweet blintzes, or the old standby buttermilk pancakes. And if you decide to order eggs instead, the good news is that most of the other breakfast platters on offer come with a short stack of pancakes too. To its credit, the Pantry offers no-yolk omelets for the health-conscious, and it's very kid-friendly as well.

The Pantry also serves lunch, which is limited to sandwiches, salads, and soups. Beware that on many weekend mornings, and some weekdays, the line for a seat at the Pantry goes out the door.

In today's retro-happy world, it isn't too hard to find an old-fashioned soda shop. But how many of them are the real thing? **Elliston Place Soda Shop** (2111 Elliston Pl., 615/327-1090, Mon.–Fri. 7 A.M.–7 P.M., Sat. 7 A.M.–5 P.M., $5–9), near Centennial Park and Vanderbilt, is one of these rare holdovers from the past, and it's proud of it. The black-and-white tile floors, lunch counter, and Purity Milk advertisements may have been here for decades, but the food is consistently fresh and good. Choose between a sandwich or a plate lunch, but be sure to save room for a classic milkshake or slice of hot pie with ice cream on top. Yum!

Nashville's original coffee shop, **Bongo Java** (2007 Belmont Blvd., 615/385-5282, Mon.–Fri. 7 A.M.–11 P.M., Sat.–Sun. 8 A.M.–11 P.M.) is just as popular as ever. Located near Belmont University, Bongo, as its frequent patrons call it, is regularly full of students chatting, texting, and surfing the Internet thanks to free wireless Internet. Set in an old house with a huge front porch, Bongo feels homey and welcoming, and a bit more on the hippie side than other Nashville coffee shops. Nonetheless, expect the latest in coffee drinks, premium salads, and sandwiches. Breakfast, including Bongo French toast, is served all day. There is a bulletin board, a good place to find and seek roommates or apartments.

Voted Nashville's favorite coffee shop, **Fido** (1812 21st Ave. S., 615/777-3436, Mon.–Fri. 7 A.M.–11 P.M., Sat. 8 A.M.–midnight, Sun. 8 A.M.–11 P.M.) near Vanderbilt is a place to see and be seen. Take a seat along the front plate-glass windows to watch the pretty people as they stroll between the Sunset Grill and Posh, one of Nashville's most upscale clothing boutiques. Fido's is a tad dark, with sleek furnishings and rock music playing. It is not unfriendly, but has a harder edge than Bongo Java. In addition to coffee, sandwiches, salads, and baked goods are also on the menu.

Said to have the best burger in Nashville, **Rotier's** (2413 Elliston Pl., 615/327-9892, Mon.–Fri. 10:30 A.M.–10 P.M., Sat. 9 A.M.–10 P.M., $5–12) is also a respected meat-and-three diner. Choose from classic sandwiches or comfort-food dinners. The Saturday breakfast will fuel you all day long. Ask about the milkshake, a city favorite that appears nowhere on the menu.

Dessert takes center stage at **Bobbie's Dairy Dip** (5301 Charlotte Ave., 615/292-2112, Mon.–Thurs. 11 A.M.–9 P.M., Fri.–Sat. 11 A.M.–10 P.M., Sun. noon–9 P.M., $4–7). The cheeseburgers and chili dogs are the comfort food you've dreamed of, and you can finish off with soft-serve ice cream, dipped cones, sundaes, and banana splits. Bobbie's closes during the winter months; call ahead to confirm they're open.

East Nashville

The most creative deli in Nashville is **Mitchell's Delicatessen** (1402 McGavock Pk., 615/262-9862, Tues.–Sat. 7 A.M.–7 P.M., Sun. 7 A.M.–4 P.M., $5–9). Order the roasted lamb and raita; a Vietnamese-style creation with pork, liver pate, and veggies; or a BLT fit for a king. Breakfast is served until 11 A.M., and there is also a daily menu of soups and hot plate specials. Stop here for top-notch bread, cheese, and meats for your own sandwiches, too.

South Nashville

Aurora Bakery and Cafe (3725 Nolensville Pike, 615/837-1993, Mon.–Sat. 7 A.M.–8 P.M., $5–6) offers one of the most cheerful welcomes among Nashville eateries. The café is clean, bright, and full of the smell of fresh baked goods. Come here to buy loaves of fresh white bread, or to sample one of the dozens of types of pastries, cookies, and cakes, many of them traditional Hispanic recipes. Specialties include empanadas and *tres leche* cake.

SOUTHERN SPECIALTIES

Downtown

Run, don't walk, to **(Arnold's Country Kitchen** (605 8th Ave. S., 615/256-4455, Mon.–Fri. 10:30 A.M.–2:45 P.M., $7–10) for some of the best Southern cooking in town. Set in a red cinder-block building on the southern outskirts of downtown, Arnold's is a food-lover's dream. No haute or fusion cuisine here—this is real food! It's set up cafeteria style, so start out by grabbing a tray while you peer at the wonders before you: chocolate pie, congealed salad (that's Jell-O to those who don't know), juicy sliced tomatoes, turnip greens, mashed potatoes, squash casserole, macaroni and cheese—and that's just the "vegetables." Choose a vegetable plate, with either three or four vegetables, or a meat-and-three for just about a buck more. Common meat dishes include ham, baked chicken, fried fish, and beef tips. All meals come with your choice of pillowy yeast rolls or cornbread. The full lunch, plus a drink, will run you under

$10. As you leave, full and happy, the only question on your mind will be, When can I come back?

Midtown

One of Nashville's most beloved meat-and-threes is **Swett's** (2725 Clifton Ave., 615/329-4418, daily 11 A.M.–8 P.M., $7–10), family owned and operated since 1954. People come from all over the city to eat at this North Nashville institution, which combines soul food and Southern cooking with great results. The food here is homemade and authentic, down to the real mashed potatoes, the vinegary greens, and the yeast rolls. Swett's is set up cafeteria style. Start by grabbing dessert—the pies are excellent—and then you move on to the good stuff: Country-fried steak, pork chops, meatloaf, fried catfish, and ham are a few of the usual suspects. A standard plate comes with one meat, two sides, and a serving of either yeast roll or cornbread, but you can add more sides if you like. Draw your own iced tea—sweet or unsweet—at the end and then find a seat, if you can.

North Nashville

Nashville's most sublime food experience is not to be found in a fine restaurant or even at a standard meat-and-three cafeteria. The food that you'll still be dreaming about when you get home is found at **(Prince's Hot Chicken Shack** (123 Ewing Dr., 615/226-9442, Tues.–Thurs. noon–10 P.M., Fri.–Sat. 2 P.M.–1 A.M., $4–6) in North Nashville. Hot chicken is skillet-fried chicken that is also spicy, and you can find hot chicken outlets in Nashville, Memphis, and a few other Southern cities. But no hot chicken shop does it quite as well as Prince's, where the hot chicken comes in three varieties: mild, hot, and extra-hot. Most uninitiated will find the mild variety pretty darn spicy, so beware. It is served with slices of white bread—perfect for soaking up that spicy chicken juice—and pickles. You can add a cup of creamy potato salad, coleslaw, or baked beans if you like. When you walk into Prince's, head to the back where you'll place your order

© SUSANNA HENIGHAN POTTER

a typical meat-and-three plate lunch, as served at Swett's

at the window, pay, and be given a number. Then take a seat—if you can find one—while you wait for your food. You can order to go or eat in. Your food is made to order, and Prince's is very popular, so the wait often exceeds 30 minutes. Have heart though—Prince's chicken is worth the wait.

West End

For a refined Southern food experience there's **Martha's at the Plantation** (5025 Harding Rd., 615/353-2828, daily 11 A.M.–2 P.M., $9–15), a sunny family-friendly café located above the gift shop at Belle Meade Plantation. Proprietor Martha Stamps offers favorites like chicken croquettes, fried chicken, and fried catfish sandwiches. Salads include cornmeal-crusted oysters on a bed of romaine, and popular side dishes are squash casserole, baked cheese grits, and spicy kale. For your main dish, try the boneless pork chop with cranberry glaze or a patty melt on sourdough toast. Her chicken and tuna salad sandwiches are also consistently good. Kids can choose from

favorites including macaroni and cheese and peanut butter and jelly sandwiches.

West of Nashville

The **Loveless Cafe** (8400 Hwy. 100, 615/646-9700, daily 7 A.M.–9 P.M., $7–13) is an institution, and some may argue it's a state of mind. But this little café-that-could is increasingly a destination too, for visitors not just to Nashville but the entire heartland of Tennessee. The Loveless got its start in 1951 when Lon and Annie Loveless started to serve good country cooking to travelers on Highway 100. Over the years the restaurant changed hands, but Annie's biscuit recipe remained the same, and it was the biscuits that kept Nashvillians, including many famous ones, coming back for more. In 1982 then owner George McCabe started the Hams & Jams mail-order business, and in 2003 the Loveless underwent a major renovation that expanded the kitchen and dining rooms and added additional shops in the rear. The food at the Loveless is good, no doubt about it. The biscuits are fluffy and buttery,

© SUSANNA HENIGHAN POTTER

The Loveless Cafe is a culinary landmark.

the ham salty, and the eggs, bacon, and sausage will hit the spot. The supper and lunch menu has expanded to include Southern standards like fried catfish and chicken, pit-cooked pork barbecue, pork chops, and meatloaf, as well as a few salads. The prices are a bit on the high side—a basic plate of bacon and eggs will run you at least $9—but a destination restaurant can do that. Parties of four or more can choose the family-style breakfast, which offers all the fruit, bacon, sausage, fries, gravy, eggs, biscuits, and preserves you can eat for $11 per adult and $6 per child. The Loveless is located about 20 miles from downtown Nashville; plan on a 30-minute drive out Highway 100. Once you get out of the clutter of West End, it's a pretty trip.

BARBECUE
Downtown

Thousands of tourists can't be wrong; **Jack's Bar-B-Que** (416 Broadway, 615/254-5715, Mon.–Thurs. 10:30 A.M.–9 P.M., Fri.–Sat. 10:30 A.M.–10 P.M., Sun. noon–6 P.M., $4–13)

is a great place to grab a bite on Broadway. Choose from barbecue pork shoulder, brisket, turkey, ribs, or sausage, and pair it with classic Southern sides like green beans, macaroni and cheese, and fried apples. Jack's serves five types of barbecue sauce, including classic Tennessee, Texas, and Kansas City. Most diners opt for a plate of one meat, two vegetables, and bread for $8–9, but if you're really hungry go for the three-meat platter for $13. Adding to the appeal of the good, affordable food is the fact that Jack's service is fast and friendly.

Midtown

Near Centennial Park and Vanderbilt, **Hog Heaven** (115 27th Ave. N., 615/329-1234, Mon.–Sat. 10 A.M.–7 P.M., $5–10) is a small yet well-known landmark for barbecue. Pulled-pork sandwiches and beef brisket are among the most popular at this mostly take-out eatery.

East Nashville

Family-operated **Dee's Q** (1000 Riverside Dr., 615/227-0024, Mon.–Thurs. 11 A.M.–9 P.M.,

Fri.–Sat. 11 A.M.–10 P.M., Sun. 11 A.M.–7 P.M., $2.50–10) serves up Memphis-style barbecue dry ribs, brisket, turkey, and chicken. He smokes his meats over hickory fire right next door to the open-air seating area. Call for winter hours.

South Nashville

Tucked on Nolensville Pike, the land of ethnic eateries, is one of Nashville's best barbecue houses. **Martin's Bar-B-Que Joint** (7215 Nolensville Pike, 615/776-1856, Tues.–Sat. 11 A.M.–8 P.M., $3.50–20.50) has pulled pork, barbecue spareribs, smoked wings, and beef brisket, plus all the side dishes you could want: coleslaw, green beans, potato salad, and the best corncakes this side of town. You can also order burgers and a mean catfish po-boy. Martin's is located inside the Nolensville city limits, about 30 minutes' drive south from downtown Nashville.

STEAKHOUSES
Downtown

Most everything about **Demos' Steak and Spaghetti House** (300 Commerce St., 615/256-4655, daily 11 A.M.–11 P.M., $6–15) is upscale except the price. Just as the name suggests, Demos' specializes in steaks and spaghetti, and it has earned a reputation among Nashville residents for quality food and good value. Choose from hamburger steak, rib eye, or sirloin, or try one of the 12 different spaghetti dinners, including seafood sauce and browned butter with garlic. The portions are more than generous, pleasing to the biggest appetites. The original Demos' is in Murfreesboro, and there are other locations in Lebanon and Hendersonville.

Midtown

◖ **Jimmy Kelly's** (217 Louise Ave., 615/329-4349, Mon.–Sat. 5 P.M.–midnight, $12–36) is a family-run old-school steakhouse. Set in an old Victorian mansion a few blocks from Centennial Park and Vanderbilt, Jimmy Kelly's has been operated by the Kelly family since 1934. During its lifetime, food fads have come and gone, but Jimmy Kelly's has

continued to serve excellent steaks and other grill foods. Dinner begins with irresistible corn cakes, and continues with classic appetizers like crab cakes or fried calamari. Entrée choices include a half-dozen different steaks, lamb, grilled chicken, and seafood, including the best blackened catfish in the city. Jimmy Kelly's offers low lighting, wood paneling, and attentive, but not fussy, service. Tables are set throughout what were once parlors, bedrooms, and porches in the old home, giving diners a feeling of homey intimacy.

CONTEMPORARY
Downtown

The thoughtful menu, careful preparations, and intimate atmosphere at the ◖ **Mad Platter** (1239 6th Ave. N., 615/242-2563, Mon.–Fri. 10 A.M.–2 P.M., Wed.–Sat. 5:30–11 P.M., Sun. 5–11 P.M., $18–29) have made it one of Nashville's favorite "nice" restaurants for years. Located among restored townhouses in the tiny Germantown neighborhood just north of the Bicentennial Mall, the Mad Platter is the work of Craig and Marcia Jervis, two chefs who met while catering the mid-1980s Michael Jackson's Victory tour. The Jervises married and opened the Mad Hatter, where they demonstrate their love for food, and each other, every day. Signature entrées include the Mad Platter rack of lamb, which is tender and juicy, and the porcini-dusted shrimp. For a special occasion, or just to enjoy one of the city's best dining deals, choose the five-course special. Add $20 to your favorite entrée and you'll get soup, appetizer, salad, and dessert, too. Talk about a meal to remember! Lunch features sandwiches, pasta, and salads for $7–13. The chicken salad is sweet and tangy, and comes with fresh banana bread. Reservations are advisable at dinner; for lunch, come early to head off the business crowd.

Rub elbows with legislators, lobbyists, and other members of the jet set at the **Capitol Grill** (23 6th Ave. N., 615/345-7116, daily 6:30 A.M.–2 P.M. and 5:30–10 P.M., $16–47). Located in the ground floor of the elegant Hermitage Hotel and set a stone's throw from

NASHVILLE

the Tennessee State Capitol, this is the sort of restaurant where marriages are proposed and deals are done. The menu is fine dining at its best: choice cuts of meat prepared with exacting care. Dinner features rack of elk, sea bass, and pork chops; the provenience of each is noted on the menu. The lunch menu is more modest, including the Capitol Grill burger, a grilled pimento cheese sandwich, and meat entrées for $11–18. The business lunch offers a lunch entrée and your choice of soup or salad for $20. Breakfast ($4–16) may be the most decadent of all, with cinnamon-swirl French toast, eggs Benedict, lobster and shirred eggs, and an array of fresh pastries and fruit. The Sunday Brunch features the best of the grill's lunch and breakfast menus, and is consistently popular.

Adjacent to the Capitol Grill is the Oak Bar, a wood-paneled and intimate bar for pre- or post-dinner drinks and conversation.

Midtown

Restaurant Zola (3001 West End Ave., 615/320-7778, Mon.–Thurs. 5:30–10 P.M., Fri.–Sat. 5:30–11 P.M., $16–30) is consistently among Nashville's favorite restaurants for romance, special occasions, and its menu. Located in a strip mall in the city's upscale West End, Restaurant Zola wows with its intriguing fusion of Mediterranean and Southern cuisine and superb wine list. Fresh seafood, top-grade meats, and vegetarian entrées that are much more than an afterthought define the menu. Zola's paella and the lobster omelet headline the seafood menu; pork tenderloin and grilled venison highlight the meats, and the signature vegetable tower will make even meat-eaters smile. Be sure to save room for some of the best desserts in town.

⟨ F. Scott's (2210 Crestmore Rd., 615/269-5861, Mon.–Thurs. 5:30–10 P.M., Fri.–Sat. 5:30–11 P.M., Sun. 5:30–9 P.M., $26–38) is an upscale restaurant and jazz bar with one of the best wine lists in Nashville. Diners are ushered into a black-and-white-tiled dining room, where the sounds of live jazz from the adjacent

listening room follow them. Enjoy a relaxed meal with wine pairings and great conversation. Food at F. Scott's is meant to be savored. Appetizers include rabbit tart, or pancetta and scallops with caviar, and entrées might be pan-seared seafood, dressed-up shepherd's pie, and grilled beef tenderloin. Save room for dessert: homemade ice cream, coconut cake, or a cheese plate paired with the perfect dessert wine.

A favorite for Music Row power lunches, special occasions, and late-night bar food, **Sunset Grill** (2001 Belcourt Ave., 615/386-3663, $11–30) serves lunch Tuesday–Friday 11 A.M.–3 P.M., dinner nightly 5–11 P.M., and late-night Monday–Saturday until 1:30 A.M. Dinner favorites include Voodoo Pasta, a spicy pasta dish with shrimp and andouille sausage, and the grilled beef tenderloin. At lunch, when most choices clock in at under $12, you can order salads, sandwiches, and pasta. The Cobb salad and chicken-salad sandwiches are always popular. Food here is prepared with care, often using organic and locally produced ingredients. The outdoor patio is popular during warm weather, and it is a great place to people-watch.

East Nashville

The Family Wash (2038 Greenwood Ave., 615/226-6070, Tues.–Sat. 6 P.M.–midnight, $9–15) is a live music listening room that serves good food at surprisingly low cost. Where else can you get a well-cooked steak for just $14? Choose from baked mac and cheese, the killer meat or vegetarian shepherd's pie, or roasted salmon and jasmine rice. Pizzas and the flank steak sandwich are always good. Reservations are accepted, and a good idea, especially when a popular musician is on the stage. The Wash, located in an old laundry, books up-and-coming singer-songwriters, and when the music is on, the conversation stops. This is a restaurant with a lot of energy and a little attitude.

ETHNIC CUISINE
Downtown

There are several Greek restaurants amid Nashville's office towers and State buildings.

One of the best is **Santorini** (210 4th Ave., 615/254-4524, Mon.–Fri. 10:30 A.M.–3 P.M., $3.50–5.75). Choose from falafel, gyro, chicken, or spinach pie, served as a plate (with rice, salad, and pita), salad (with pita, tabouli, and salad), or meal (with fries). The food is fresh and well prepared, and the premises are neat and clean.

Located in the downtown Arcade, **House of Pizza** (15 Arcade, 615/242-7144, Mon.–Fri. 10 A.M.–6 P.M., Sat. 11 A.M.–4:30 P.M.) serves up thick- and thin-crust varieties, massive stromboli, mighty lasagna, and huge meatball subs. The restaurant is small; eating in can be a challenge, especially since Nashvillians flock here for the best pizza in town.

Midtown

The venerable **International Market and Restaurant** (2010 Belmont Blvd., 615/297-4453, daily 10:30 A.M.–9 P.M., $4–10) near Belmont University and Hillsboro Village may well be the best choice for a cheap lunch in Nashville. The cafeteria serves lots of vegetable, noodle, and rice dishes, many of them Thai in origin, at prices that seem not to have risen much since the restaurant was established in 1975. If you want to splurge, order a "from the kitchen" special of pad thai or another dish, which will be made from scratch just for you.

For the best Italian food in Nashville, head west to the neighborhood of Sylvan Park, where you'll find **Caffe Nonna** (4427 Murphy Rd., 615/463-0133, Tues.–Fri. 11 A.M.–2 P.M., Mon.–Thurs. 5–9 P.M., Fri.–Sat. 5–10 P.M., $12–21). Inspired by chef Daniel Maggipinto's own Nonna (grandmother), the café serves rustic Italian fare. Appetizers include salads and bruschetta and entrées include the divine Lasagne Nonna, made with butternut squash, ricotta cheese, spinach, and sage. One of the best deals is the mix-and-match pasta; choose your own pasta and sauce for $10 at lunch and $12 at dinner. The lunch menu offers a dozen different sandwiches, including basil chicken salad and Italian-fried tilapia, for under $10. The

service at Caffe Nonna is friendly and attentive, and the atmosphere is cozy.

Located just west of the Kroger food store and on the opposite side of the street, K&S World Market on Charlotte Avenue, the second in a chain whose original location is on Nolensville Pike, will keep any foodie happy for hours with its obscure and unusual food items. In the same shopping center you'll find Nashvillians' favorite Vietnamese restaurant, **Kien Giang** (5825 Charlotte Ave., 615/353-1250, Tues.–Fri. 11 A.M.–9 P.M., Sat.–Sun. 10 A.M.–9 P.M., $4–12).

Drive a bit farther out to find **La Hispana Panaderia** (6208 Charlotte Pike, 615/352-3798, daily 6 A.M.–9 P.M.), whose bread and pastries are as good as the finest European bakery but at a fraction of the cost.

One of Nashville's oldest Indian restaurants, **Shalimar** (3711 Hillsboro Rd., 615/269-8577, Mon.–Sat. 11 A.M.–10 P.M., $11–17) offers fine food and efficient service. The $11 lunch combo of entrée, rice, naan, salad, and a drink is popular, along with the Saturday lunch buffet. At dinner, Shalimar takes on a slightly more elegant cast with vegetarian, chicken, lamb, and seafood entrées in popular preparations including masala, biryani, tikka, saag, or korma. Shalimar is a few blocks away from the Green Hills Mall.

South Nashville

Chosen by Nashvillians as the best Mexican restaurant in a very crowded field, **La Hacienda Taqueria** (2615 Nolensville Pike, 615/256-6142, Mon.–Thurs. 10 A.M.–9 P.M., Fri. 10 A.M.–10 P.M., Sat. 9 A.M.–10 A.M., Sun. 9 A.M.–9 P.M., $2–14) is located within a colorful storefront on Nolensville Pike, Nashville's most ethnically diverse thoroughfare. The menu offers a dizzying array of choices—tacos, enchiladas, tamales, burritos, quesadillas, and *tortas,* just to name a few. Most come with your choice of chicken, chorizo, tripe, pork, or steak filling, and many have an authenticity often missing from Mexican restaurant fare. Combination platters, which offer three items plus rice and beans, are a good way to sample the options if you aren't sure what to order.

If you aren't in the mood for Mexican, just drive a bit farther along Nolensville Pike for other choices. Among them is **Dunya Kebob** (2521 Nolensville Pike, 615/242-6664, Mon.–Thurs. 11 A.M.–9:30 P.M., Fri.–Sat. 11 A.M.–10:30 P.M., Sun. noon–9:30 P.M., $5–10), which offers chicken, lamb, beef, and seafood kebobs and gyro sandwiches.

Not far from Nolensville, you'll find two more international favorites in the same shopping center on Trousdale Drive. **Back to Cuba** (4683 Trousdale Dr., 615/837-6711, Tues.–Sat. 11 A.M.–9 P.M., $8–12) serves traditional Cuban favorites: Grilled sandwiches of pork, ham, cheese, and pickle are a popular choice at lunchtime. For dinner, try the roast pork or grilled shrimp and don't skip the lacy fried plantains and spicy black beans.

For homemade Italian fare, go to **Mama Mia's** (4501 Trousdale Dr., 615/331-7207, Mon.–Fri. 11 A.M.–2 P.M., Mon.–Sat. 5–10 P.M., $7–16), which offers lasagna, ravioli, chicken, veal, and seafood dishes. Bring your own wine.

MARKETS

For fresh fruits, vegetables, preserves, and honey, go to the **Nashville Farmer's Market** held daily in the large covered building between 8th Avenue and the Bicentennial Mall. Many of the goods for sale here are home-

© SUSANNA HENIGHAN POTTER

Fresh vegetables are on sale at the Nashville Farmer's Market on 8th Avenue.

grown at farms near Nashville; to be sure, ask whether you're getting Tennessee products.

There is an abundance of traditional grocery stores around Nashville. Common chains are Kroger, Publix, and H. G. Hill. Drive out any of the main corridors into the city and you will quickly find a grocery store. There is a Trader Joe's, which specializes in organic and specialty items, in Green Hills, just south of the Green Hills Mall.

Information and Services

INFORMATION

Visitors Centers

The main visitors center (615/259-4747, Mon.–Sat. 8 A.M.–5 P.M., Sun. 10 A.M.–5 P.M.) is located at the corner of 5th Avenue and Broadway, inside the Nashville Arena. Here you can pick up brochures, get a free map, and find answers to just about any question. It is open late when there is an event at the Nashville Arena.

There is another visitors center a few blocks uptown at 1 Nashville Place (615/259-4730, Mon.–Fri. 8 A.M.–5 P.M.).

Maps

Visitors centers offer a free hand-out map of downtown and an area map that shows major thoroughfares. This will be sufficient for many travelers. However, if you plan to do a lot of driving or off-the-beaten-track exploring, pick up a city map such as those published by Rand McNally or AAA. Detailed maps may be purchased from local drugstores and bookstores. Save time by buying a map before you arrive.

Media

NEWSPAPERS

Nashville's daily morning broadsheet is the *Tennessean* (www.tennessean.com). Published under various names since 1812, the *Tennessean* offers what every big-city newspaper does: local, regional, and national news, plus lots more. The paper's entertainment insert is published with the Friday newspaper. The newspaper is available all over town for 50 cents on weekdays and Saturdays, $1.75 on Sundays.

The *City Paper* (www.nashvillecitypaper.com) is a free twice-weekly tabloid with a strong website that specializes in local news, sports, and events. It offers an alternative viewpoint to that of the *Tennessean* and makes a good, compact read for locals and visitors. You can pick up *City Paper* in dozens of downtown locations.

The *Nashville Scene* is a fat tabloid-sized alternative weekly that balances its coverage of the local arts, music, and social scene with some political and local news coverage. This is a good go-to choice to understand what's going on in the city. *All the Rage,* owned by the *Tennessean,* is also published on Thursdays and focuses solely on entertainment and events.

Nashville Music Guide (www.nashvillemusicguide.com) is a free tabloid published twice a month. It covers the local music scene and music-industry news.

In addition, the *Nashville Business Journal* (615/248-2222, $1) is a weekly business publication covering industry, commerce, and finance. It is distributed on Mondays. *Nashville Pride* (615/292-9150, $0.50) covers African-American news and is distributed on Fridays.

Also published by the *Tennessean,* *Nashville Lifestyles* is a monthly magazine with local celebrity profiles, home and garden tips, event information, and advertising. You can pick it up at newsstands throughout the city.

American Songwriter Magazine (1303 16th Ave. S., 615/321-6069, www.americansongwriter.com) is a bimonthly magazine devoted to the art of songwriting. It has been published in Nashville since 1984.

RADIO

The Nashville dial is chock-a-block with the usual commercial radio prospects. There are a few radio stations worth mentioning, however. **WSM 650 AM** is the legendary radio station that started it all when it put a fiddler on the air in 1925. Still airing the Grand Ole Opry after all these years, WSM plays country music at other times.

Nashville Public Radio is **WPLN 90.3 FM.** Tune in here for classical music and National Public Radio news. **WPLN 1430 AM** is a companion station with all-day news and talk, including BBC broadcasts. Nashville's only community radio station is **Radio Free Nashville** (98.9 FM, www.radiofreenashville.org). While its signal only reaches a small part of the city now, Radio Free Nashville is looking to expand its reach as soon as it raises the necessary funds.

WKDA 900 AM is Nashville's Spanish-language radio station. **WAMB 1160 AM** plays big-band music, and **WNAH 1360 AM** plays old-fashioned Southern gospel.

Several Nashville universities liven up the radio dial. Fisk's **WFSK 88.1 FM** plays jazz. Middle Tennessee State University has **WMTS 88.3 FM,** the student-run station, and **WMOT 89.5 FM,** a jazz station. Vanderbilt University's student radio station is **WRVU 91.1 FM.**

TELEVISION

Nashville's network affiliates offer local news morning and night. These include **WKRN** (Channel 2 ABC), **WSMV** (Channel 4 NBC), **WTVF** (Channel 5 CBS), and **WZTV** (Channel 17 FOX).

The local public-television station is **WNPT** (Channel 8 PBS).

Remember that since Nashville is in the Central time zone, most nationally televised programs air one hour earlier than they do on the East Coast.

SERVICES
Internet

You can go online free at the **Nashville Public Library** (615 Church St., 615/862-5800). There is free wireless access at the visitors center located at 5th and Broadway.

Postal Service

Mail a letter or buy stamps from the downtown post offices at 901 Broadway and 1718 Church Street. Both are open Monday–Friday 8:30 A.M.–5 P.M. There is also a post office in the downtown Arcade.

Emergency Services

Dial 911 for police, fire, or ambulance in an emergency. For help with a traffic accident, call the Tennessee Highway Patrol at 615/741-2060. The Davidson County Rescue Squad can be summoned by calling 615/226-0462.

Libraries

Nashville's downtown library is the crown jewel of its library system. The **Nashville Public Library** (615 Church St., 615/862-5800, www.library.nashville.org, Mon.–Fri. 9 A.M.–8 P.M., Fri. 9 A.M.–6 P.M., Sat. 9 A.M.–5 P.M., Sun. 2–5 P.M.) opened in 2001, replacing an older library that had served the city since 1965. The new library is dynamic and busy serving its community. There are story hours, children's programs, art exhibits, a local history collection, and meeting rooms. Visitors to the city will find the public Internet access and wireless Internet network most useful. There is a nice courtyard inside the library where people eat lunch, relax, and enjoy occasional concerts.

If you are visiting the library, you can park in the Nashville Public Library Parking Garage. Enter on 6th or 7th Avenues between Church and Commerce Streets. The first hour of library parking is free, and the daily maximum is $6. Be sure to validate your ticket at the security desk as you enter the library.

Getting There and Around

GETTING THERE
By Air

Nashville International Airport (BNA; 615/275-1675, www.nashintl.com) is located eight miles east of the city center. To get downtown from the airport, head west on I-40; it's a short 15-minute drive. One-way taxi fare from the airport to most hotels is $22.

AIRPORT SHUTTLE

ShuttleMax (615/361-6184 or 888/500-7629, www.shuttlemax.net) provides regular shuttle service from the airport to hotels in Brentwood, Franklin, and the Opryland area. One-way fare is between $11 and $30, depending on the location of your hotel. Round-trip is between $20 and $50. Reservations are highly recommended.

Gray Line Transportation (615/883-5555, www.graylinenashville.com) offers regular shuttle service from the airport to downtown, West End, and Music Valley hotels. The shuttle departs from the airport every 15–20 minutes between 5 A.M. and 11 P.M.; reservations are not required. Call ahead to book your hotel pick-up. Fare is $11 one-way and $18 round-trip.

By Car

Driving is the most popular way to get to Nashville. The city is 250 miles from Atlanta, 330 miles from St. Louis, 400 miles from Charlotte, 550 miles from New Orleans, and 670 miles from Washington, D.C.

No less than three major interstate highways converge in Nashville. I-40 runs east–west, connecting Nashville with Knoxville and Memphis. I-65 runs north–south, and connects the city with Louisville, Kentucky, and Birmingham, Alabama. I-24 travels at a southeastern angle down to the city, connecting it with the cities of Clarkesville and St. Louis in the north, and Chattanooga and Atlanta in the south.

By Bus

Greyhound (800/231-2222, www.greyhound. com) serves Nashville with bus service to the city from Memphis, Jackson, Chattanooga, and Knoxville, Tennessee, as well as Paducah and Bowling Green, Kentucky. The Greyhound station (200 8th Ave. S., 615/255-3556) is on the southern end of downtown Nashville.

Expect to pay about $40 for a one-way ticket from Memphis to Nashville.

GETTING AROUND
Driving

The best way to get around Nashville is by car. Although visitors staying downtown will be able to find plenty to do and places to eat all within walking distance, many of the best attractions are located outside of the city center. So unless your stay is but a few days, it is best to bring or rent a car to get around.

If you don't bring your own, a dozen different major rental agencies have a fleet of cars,

trucks, and SUVs at the airport. Agencies include **Alamo** (615/361-7467, www.alamo.com), **Avis** (615/361-1212, www.avis.com), and **Hertz** (615/361-3131, www.hertz.com). For the best rates, use an online travel search tool, such as Expedia (www.expedia.com) or Travelocity (www.travelocity.com), and book the car early, along with your airline tickets.

NAVIGATING NASHVILLE

Nashville is quite easy to navigate. I-65 and I-24 create a tight inner beltway that encircles the heart of the city. I-440 is an outer beltway that circles the southern half of the city. Briley Parkway, shown on maps as Highway 155, is a limited-access highway that circles the northern outskirts of the city.

City residents use the interstates not just for long journeys but for short cross-town jaunts as well. Most businesses give directions according to the closest interstate exit.

Non-interstate thoroughfares emanate out from Nashville like spokes in a wheel. Many are named for the communities that they eventually run into. Murfreesboro Pike runs southeast from the city; Hillsboro Pike (Rte. 431) starts out as 21st Avenue South and takes you to Hillsboro Village and Green Hills. Broadway becomes West End Avenue and takes you directly to Belle Meade and, eventually, the Loveless Café. It does not take long to realize that roads in Nashville have a bad habit of changing names all of a sudden, so be prepared and check the map to avoid getting too confused.

For real-time traffic advisories and road construction closures, dial 511 from any touchtone phone, or go to www.tn511.com.

PARKING

There is metered parking on most downtown streets, but some have prohibited-parking signs effective during morning and afternoon rush hours. Always read the fine print carefully.

There is plenty of off-street parking in lots and garages. Expect to pay about $10 a day for garage parking. Meters are free after noon on Saturday, and on Sunday and holidays.

Public Transportation

Nashville's **Metropolitan Transit Authority** operates city buses. Pick up a map and schedule from either of the two downtown visitors centers, or online at www.nashvillemta.org.

Few tourists ride the buses because they can be difficult to understand if you're new to the city, and because they are not the most efficient use of your time. One route that is helpful, however, is the Opry Mills Express that travels from downtown Nashville to Music Valley, home of the Grand Ole Opry, Opryland Hotel, and Opry Mills, a shopping mall. The Opry Mills Express departs the Nashville Arena 13 times a day on weekdays. Fare is $1.75 one way; $0.60 for senior citizens. You can pick up a detailed route timetable from either of the two downtown visitors centers.

On Tennessee Titans' game days, the MTA offers its End Zone Express. Park at either Greer Stadium (where the Nashville Sounds play) or the State employee lot at 4th Avenue North and Harrison, and for just $6 you get shuttled straight to LP Field.

COMMUTER RAIL

In 2006 Nashville debuted the **Music City Star Rail** (501 Union St., 615/862-8833, www.musiccitystar.org), a commuter rail system designed to ease congestion around the city. With service Monday through Friday, three morning trains and three afternoon trains connect Donelson, Hermitage, Mt. Juliet, and Lebanon to downtown Nashville. More routes are planned for the future.

One-way tickets can be purchased for $5 each from vending machines at any of the stations. You can pre-purchase single-trip tickets, 10-trip packs, and monthly passes at the Regional Transportation Authority Office at 501 Union Street Monday–Friday 10 A.M.–2 P.M. For a complete list of ticket outlets, contact the railway.

Taxis

Licensed taxicabs will have an orange driver permit, usually displayed on the visor or dashboard.

Several good cab companies are **Allied Cab Company** (615/244-7433 or 625/320-9083), **Checker Cab** (615/256-7000), **Music City Taxi Inc.** (615/262-0451, www.musiccitytaxi.com), and **United Cab** (615/228-6969).

If cruising around in a stretch limo is more your style, call **Basic Black Limo** (615/430-8157, www.basicblacklimo.net). The rate is $125 per hour on Saturday nights; the limo seats up to 14 passengers.

OUTSIDE NASHVILLE

The countryside surrounding Nashville invites exploration. The scenes are familiar: winding country roads, cutting through horse pasture; perfectly fried chicken, served with the nonchalance of someone who knows just how good it is; and charming old railroad towns, where the trains still run.

But there are other attractions that just might surprise you: an 1850s homestead, a celebration dedicated to the lowly mule, and some of the best shopping in the whole state of Tennessee. The heartland of Tennessee is a landscape of natural beauty, notable history, and some outstanding stories that will captivate its visitors.

PLANNING YOUR TIME

Franklin may be one of the most popular daytrip destinations from Nashville. It is close—a mere 20 miles down the interstate—but a world apart. The historic Carnton Plantation is the best place to learn about the Battle of Franklin; downtown Franklin is the best place to shop.

The best-known excursion from Nashville is Lynchburg, where Jack Daniel's Tennessee Whisky is made. But the best distillery tour is at the George Dickel Distillery a few miles up the road and light years apart. There are no tour buses, just the fresh country air of Cascade Hollow. On your way, stop at the charming railroad towns of Bell Buckle and Wartrace for shopping, sightseeing, and good country cooking.

Go to Land Between the Lakes for outdoor adventure and to see The Homeplace, a living-history museum that depicts frontier life in

PHOTO COURTESY THE TENNESSEE DEPARTMENT OF TOURIST DEVELOPMENT

HIGHLIGHTS

◖ **Carnton Plantation:** Let your imagination live at this mansion, which served as a Confederate field hospital during the Battle of Franklin. It is the setting of the novel *The Widow of the South* (page 86).

◖ **George Dickel Distillery:** Tennessee whiskey is world-famous, but you can beat the crowds at this lesser-known distillery in beautiful Cascade Hollow (page 97).

◖ **Tennessee Museum of Early Farm Life:** Celebrate the ingenuity and relentless work ethic of generations gone at this museum in Spring Hill (page 107).

◖ **Ancestral Home of James Knox Polk:** Boost your James K. Polk IQ at the only surviving home – besides the White House – where he lived (page 109).

◖ **The Homeplace:** Located in beautiful Land Between the Lakes, this living-history museum depicts the farmer's way of life at the mid-point of the 19th century (page 112).

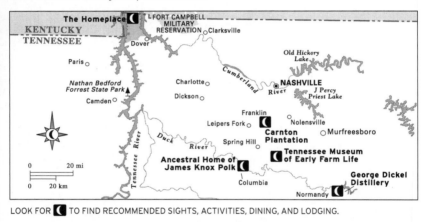

LOOK FOR ◖ TO FIND RECOMMENDED SIGHTS, ACTIVITIES, DINING, AND LODGING.

Tennessee. Or take a drive down the Natchez Trace Parkway. Say yes to inviting detours to towns like Leiper's Fork and Spring Hill, where you can visit the Tennessee Museum of Early Farm Life. Brush up on your presidential history in Columbia at the Ancestral Home of James Knox Polk, the eleventh president of the United States.

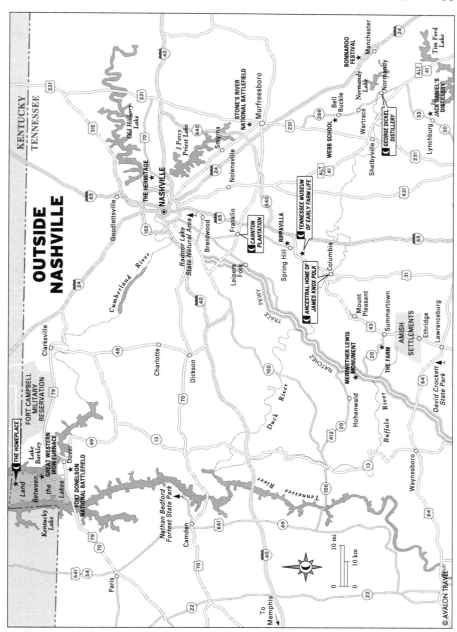

OUTSIDE NASHVILLE

KENTUCKY
TENNESSEE

THE HOMEPLACE
FORT CAMPBELL MILITARY RESERVATION
GREAT WESTERN IRON FURNACE
Lake Barkley
Dover
Land Between the Lakes
Kentucky Lake
FORT DONELSON NATIONAL BATTLEFIELD
Nathan Bedford Forrest State Park
Camden
Paris
Clarksville
Charlotte
Dickson
Duck River
Tennessee River
Waynesboro
Hohenwald
MERIWETHER LEWIS MONUMENT
THE FARM
AMISH SETTLEMENTS
Summertown
Mount Pleasant
Lawrenceburg
Ethridge
David Crockett State Park
NATCHEZ TRACE PKWY
Buffalo River
Columbia
ANCESTRAL HOME OF JAMES KNOX POLK
Spring Hill
RIPPAVILLA
TENNESSEE MUSEUM OF EARLY FARM LIFE
CARNTON PLANTATION
Franklin
Leipers Fork
Brentwood
Radnor Lake State Natural Area
NASHVILLE
THE HERMITAGE
Goodlettsville
Cumberland River
Old Hickory Lake
J Percy Priest Lake
Nolensville
Smyrna
Murfreesboro
STONE'S RIVER NATIONAL BATTLEFIELD
Shelbyville
WEBB SCHOOL
Bell Buckle
Wartrace
GEORGE DICKEL DISTILLERY
Normandy
Normandy Lake
BONNAROO FESTIVAL
Manchester
Tim Ford Lake
Lynchburg
JACK DANIEL'S DISTILLERY

To Memphis

10 mi
10 km

© AVALON TRAVEL

Franklin

Located a mere 20 miles south of Nashville, Franklin is one of the most picturesque small towns in Tennessee. It has preserved its Civil War heritage and is emerging as one of the state's best destinations for shopping.

SIGHTS

Contained within four square blocks, downtown Franklin consists of residential streets with old and carefully restored homes. The business district runs along West Main Street and includes professional offices, restaurants, and boutiques. The center of town is a traffic circle, crowned by a simple white Confederate monument. The circle is fronted by banks, more offices, and the 1859 Williamson County courthouse.

The best way to explore downtown Franklin is on foot. Free parking is available along the streets or in two public lots, one on 2nd Avenue and one on 4th Avenue. Pick up a printed walking-tour guide from the visitors center on East Main Street.

Guided walking tours of Franklin are offered by **Franklin on Foot** (615/400-3808, www.franklinonfoot.com). The classic Franklin tour provides an overview of the history of the town and its buildings. The Widow of the South Tour is combined with admission to the Carnton Plantation and is a must for lovers of that popular novel. Other tours include a children's tour and haunted Franklin tour. Tours cost between $5 and $18 per person.

McLemore House

Five generations of the McLemore family lived in the white clapboard home at the corner of Glass Street and 11th Avenue in downtown Franklin. McLemore House was built in 1880 by Harvey McLemore, a former slave and farmer. Inside, a small museum has been created that documents the story of African Americans in Williamson County.

McLemore House is open by appointment only. Contact Mary Mills at 615/794-2270 or the Convention and Visitors Bureau to arrange a tour.

◖ Carnton Plantation

When Robert Hicks's novel *The Widow of the South* became a bestseller in 2005, the staff at the Carnton Plantation (1345 Carnton Ln., 615/794-0903, www.carnton.org, Mon.–Sat. 9 A.M.–5 P.M., Sun. 1–5 P.M., $3–8) noticed an uptick in the number of visitors. The novel is a fictionalized account of Carrie McGavock and how her home, the Carnton Plantation, became a Confederate hospital during the Battle of Franklin in the Civil War.

The Carnton mansion was built in 1826 by Randal McGavock, a former Nashville mayor and prominent lawyer and businessman. Randal had died by the time of the Civil War, and it was his son, John, and John's wife, Carrie, who witnessed the bloody Battle of Franklin on November 30, 1864.

The Carnton Plantation in Franklin was made famous by the novel *The Widow of the South*.

OUTSIDE NASHVILLE

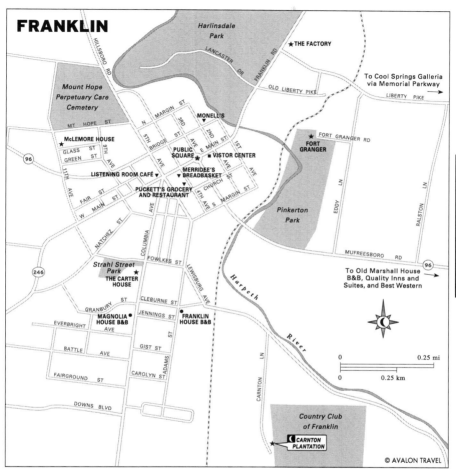

FRANKLIN

Harlinsdale Park

★ THE FACTORY

To Cool Springs Galleria via Memorial Parkway

Mount Hope Perpetuary Care Cemetery

MONELL'S ▼

McLEMORE HOUSE ★

★ FORT GRANGER RD

FORT GRANGER

PUBLIC SQUARE

■ VISTOR CENTER ★

MERRIDEE'S ▼ BREADBASKET

LISTENING ROOM CAFÉ ▼

PUCKETT'S GROCERY AND RESTAURANT

Pinkerton Park

Strahl Street Park ★ THE CARTER HOUSE

To Old Marshall House B&B, Quality Inns and Suites, and Best Western

MAGNOLIA ● HOUSE B&B

● FRANKLIN HOUSE B&B

Harpeth River

Country Club of Franklin

CARNTON PLANTATION ★

0   0.25 mi
0   0.25 km

© AVALON TRAVEL

Located behind the Confederate line, the Carnton Plantation became a hospital for hundreds of injured and dying Confederate soldiers. As late as six months after the battle, the McGavock home remained a refuge for recovering veterans.

In the years that followed the battle, the McGavocks raised money, donating much of it themselves, to construct a cemetery for the Confederate dead, and donated two acres of land to the cause.

Visitors to the Carnton Plantation can pay full price for a guided tour of the mansion and self-guided tour of the grounds, which include a smokehouse, slave house, and garden. You can also pay $3 for the self-guided tour of the grounds. There is no admission charged to visit the cemetery.

Fort Granger

An unsung attraction, Fort Granger is a lovely and interesting place to spend an hour or so.

OUTSIDE NASHVILLE

THE SOUTH'S LAST STAND

In the waning days of the Confederacy, its president, Jefferson Davis, met with his commanders to plan strategy. It was September 1864, and the Federals were pushing southward in Virginia and Georgia.

The plan that Davis and his commanders, including Gen. John Bell Hood, agreed was a daring march northward through Middle Tennessee. It was hoped that Gen. Hood's Army of the Tennessee would draw Federal forces away from the battles elsewhere and that they would eventually be repelled from the South entirely.

The last-ditch plan failed, and cost the Confederacy some 13,500 lives. The battles of Spring Hill, Franklin, and Nashville were major blows to the Southern cause and its last losing stratagem.

COURTESY OF LIBRARY OF CONGRESS

an unidentified Confederate soldier

SPRING HILL

On November 29, 1864, Gen. John M. Schofield and his federal troops were stationed in Columbia. Moving northward, Hood went around Columbia and headed towards Spring Hill. From here, Hood could either have marched to Nashville ahead of the Federals or returned to Columbia and attacked them from the rear. It was a promising position.

But the opportunity was squandered when the Confederates camped just short of a critical road northward. Schofield, who suspected Hood's strategy and realized his grave error, moved his men in the dead of night and marched them safely northward, passing within "talking distance" of the encamped Southern army.

Explanations for Hood's mistake suggest that he was not himself on that day. He was probably in tremendous physical pain from earlier war injuries (Hood had already lost the use of his left arm and had his right leg amputated below the hip), and was probably taking opium. He may also have been drunk. If walls could talk, the ones at Oaklawn on Denning Lane in Spring Hill, an 1835 mansion that served as the Confederate headquarters, would have a tale to tell.

Built between 1862 and 1863 by Union forces, the earthenwork fort is set on a bluff overlooking the Harpeth River just south of downtown Franklin. The fort was the largest fortification in the area built by Captain W. E. Merrill during the Federal occupation of Franklin. It saw action twice in 1863 and also in 1864 during the Battle of Franklin.

Many features of the fort remain intact for today's visitors. You can walk around portions of the breastworks. The interior of the fort is now a grassy field, perfect for a summer picnic or game of catch. An overlook at one end of the fort provides an unmatched view of the surrounding countryside.

You can reach Fort Granger two ways. One is along a short but steep trail departing Pinkerton Park on Murfreesboro Road east of town. Or you can drive straight to the fort by heading out of town on East Main Street. Turn right onto Liberty Pike, right onto Eddy Lane, and, finally, right again onto Fort Granger Drive.

The fort, which is maintained by the City of Franklin, is open during daylight hours only. While there is no office or visitors center at the

Whatever the cause, on the morning of November 30, when Hood realized what had happened, he resolved to battle the Federals in Franklin. Fueled by shame and desperation, Hood ordered the charge at the Battle of Franklin, one of the South's bloodiest defeats of the war.

FRANKLIN

By the time Hood and his army reached Franklin on November 30, 1864, the general was frustrated and the men exhausted. The missed opportunity at Spring Hill stung, but worse was yet to come.

Ignoring the advice of his commanders, including Nathan Bedford Forrest and Benjamin Franklin Cheatham, Hood ordered a full frontal attack on the federal line around Franklin. Unlike many other battles of the Civil War, the troops at Franklin had a full view at each other. There were some 23,000 Federal soldiers on one side, and 20,000 Confederates on the other. At about 4 P.M. on the last day of November, 1864, 18 brigades of Confederate soldiers, many of them from Tennessee, marched towards the Federal line. With the rebel yell that made them famous, the attack had begun. It was like sending soldiers to the slaughter.

It was a bloody and fierce battle. Even those commanders and soldiers on the Confederate side who had doubts about the battle strategy fought bravely and often to the death. The hand-to-hand combat around the Carter

House near downtown Franklin was some of the fiercest of the battle. One Federal soldier said that the fighting was in such close quarters that "even the poorest marksman could not fail to hit a human target."

The Confederate assault failed. The fighting ended around 9 P.M. and overnight Federal Gen. John M. Schofield and all his soldiers who could walk marched to Nashville. They left their dead on the battlefield. Two weeks later, they defeated Hood's army again during the Battle of Nashville.

The death toll at Franklin was staggering. Some 7,000 Confederate were killed, wounded, or captured in just five hours of battle. The Federals lost 2,500 men. Many injured warriors died on the battlefield overnight, when temperatures dropped below freezing.

The townspeople of Franklin were left to tend to the wounded on both sides of the battle. Nearly every home in the city became a makeshift hospital. The most famous of these was the Carnton Plantation, where visitors today can still see blood stains on the floor, left by injured and dying soldiers.

In 1866, John and Carrie McGavock established a Confederate cemetery on the grounds of Carnton. It holds 1,500 graves, making it the largest private military cemetery in the nation. Carrie kept a careful record of the men who were buried there, and her cemetery book was used by thousands of people who came to Franklin to mourn loved ones who died there.

OUTSIDE NASHVILLE

fort, you may contact Franklin's parks department (615/794-2103) for more information.

The Carter House

Some of the fiercest fighting in the Battle of Franklin took place around the farm and house belonging to the Carter family on the outskirts of town. The family took refuge in the basement while Union and Confederate soldiers fought hand to hand right above them. Today, the Carter House (1140 Columbia Ave., 615/791-1861, www.carter-house.org, Mon.–Sat. 9 A.M.–5 P.M., Sun. 1–5 P.M., adults $8, seniors $7, children 7–13 $4)

is the best place to come for a detailed examination of the battle and the profound human toll that it exacted on both sides.

You will see hundreds of bullet holes, which help to illustrate the ferocity of the fight. Guides describe some of the worst moments of the battle, and bring to life a few of the people who fought it. The house also holds a museum of Civil War uniforms and memorabilia, including photographs and short biographies of many of the men who were killed in Franklin. There is also a video about the battle, which shows scenes from a reenactment.

ENTERTAINMENT
Theater
The **Boiler Room Theatre** (The Factory, 615/794-7744, www.boilerroomtheatre.com) is a professional theater company that performs seven or eight productions each year. Shows take place in a 120-seat theater in building six at the Factory (see *Shopping*), and range from light-hearted musical theater to dramas. The theater's season runs year-round.

Live Music
The **Listening Room Cafe** (500 W. Main St., 615/591-5725) hosts in-the-round and other intimate concerts several nights a week. Songwriters and musicians from Nashville frequently head down here for a night's show, which typically begins around 7 P.M.

SHOPPING
In many respects, shopping is Franklin's greatest attraction. Trendy downtown shops, the unique environment of the Factory, and proximity to a major mall make this a destination for shoppers. It is also one of Tennessee's most popular antiques shopping destinations.

Antiques
Franklin declares itself "the new antiques capital of Tennessee." Indeed, antiquing is one of the most popular pursuits of Franklin's visitors, and at least two dozen antiques shops serve to quench the thirst for something old. The town's antiques district is huddled around the corner of Margin Street and 2nd Avenue. Here you'll find no less than six major antiques stores. Other shops are found along Main Street in the downtown shopping district.

The best place to start antiquing is the **Franklin Antique Mall** (251 2nd Ave. S., 615/790-8593), located in the town's old ice house. The mall is a maze of rooms, each with different goods on offer. Possibilities include books, dishware, quilts, furniture, knick-knacks, and housewares. You can also follow 5th Avenue about two blocks south of downtown to find **Country Charm Antique Mall** (301 Lewisburg Ave., 615/790-8998),

whose three buildings house a vast array of furniture, quilts, glassware, china, and home decor.

Just outside the Franklin Antique Mall are at least five other antiques shops to roam through, including **J. J. Ashley's** (125 S. Margin St., 615/791-0011), which specializes in French and English Country accessories, as well as European furniture. **Scarlett Scales Antiques** (212 S. Margin St., 615/791-4097), located in a 1900s shotgun house, has American country furnishings, accessories, and architectural elements arriving daily.

Downtown
Retail is alive and well in Franklin's downtown. West Main Street is the epicenter of the shopping district, although you will find stores scattered around other parts of downtown as well. Home decor, classy antiques, trendy clothes, and specialty items like candles, tea, and gardening supplies are just a few of the things you'll find in downtown Franklin.

Most shops in downtown Franklin are open by 10 A.M. and many stay open until the evening to catch late-afternoon visitors. You can easily navigate the downtown shopping district on foot, although you may need to stow your parcels in the car now and then.

Bink's Outfitters (421 Main St., 615/599-8777) sells outdoor clothing and equipment. Stylish ladies' apparel and accessories are sold at **Chico's** (348 Main St., 615/599-8471). Go to **ENJOUE** (400 Main St., 615/599-8177) for funky fashions and trendy styles.

The city's best bookstore is **Landmark Booksellers** (114 E. Main St., 615/791-6400), found on the other side of the town square. They have a wide selection of used and new books, including many regional titles. It is friendly and welcoming, with fresh coffee for sale in the mornings.

Franklin Tea Merchant (430 Main St., 615/794-6311) has a wide selection of loose tea and various tea accessories. Toys old and new are on sale at **Main Street Toy Co.** (412 Main St., 615/790-4869). For the best in paper, wrappings, and stationery, go to **Rock Paper**

Scissors (317 Main St., 615/791-0150). **Heart and Hands** (418 Main St., 615/794-2537) is one of several shops specializing in crafts and home decor.

The Factory

Franklin's most unique retail center is the Factory (230 Franklin Rd., 615/791-1777, www.factoryatfranklin.com). A 250,000-square-foot complex of 11 different old industrial buildings, the Factory once housed stove factories and a textile mill. In the mid-1990s, Calvin Lehew bought the dilapidated eyesore and began the lengthy process of restoring the buildings and converting them to a space for galleries, retail shops, restaurants, and other businesses.

Today, the Factory is a vibrant commercial center for the city of Franklin. It houses a refreshing array of local independent retailers, including galleries, salons, candy shops, and a pet boutique. **The Little Cottage** (615/794-1405) sells children's fashions. Quilting supplies and fabric are the mainstays at **The Smocking Loft** (615/794-6226).

There are also 11 different studios and learning centers, including the **Viking Store** (615/599-9617), which offers cooking demonstrations and classes; **Creation Station** (615/791-9192), where you can practice scrapbooking; and **Arts for Life** (615/995-2778), which offers art classes and music lessons. There are also talent agencies and a Taekwondo academy.

In addition to retail and learning centers, the Factory has four restaurants and a fish market.

Cool Springs Galleria

Cool Springs Galleria (1800 Galleria Blvd., Cool Springs, 615/771-2128, www.coolspringsgalleria.com) is a mall with 165 specialty stores, 5 major department stores, 20 restaurants, and a 500-seat food court. It is located a few miles north of Franklin, convenient to I-65. Shops include Zales, Wild Oats, Talbots, Pier 1, Pottery Barn, Macy's, JC Penney, and Eddie Bauer. The mall is found at exits 68B and 69 on I-65.

ACCOMMODATIONS
Under $100

Several chain motels surround the interstate near Franklin. Closest to town are the 89-room **Quality Inns and Suites** (1307 Murfreesboro Rd., 615/794-7591, $65–110) and the 142-room **Best Western** (1308 Murfreesboro Rd., 615/790-0570, $55–70). Both offer wireless Internet, free continental breakfast, and an outdoor pool.

$100-150

The **Magnolia House Bed and Breakfast** (1317 Columbia Ave., 615/794-8178, www.bbonline.com/tn/magnolia, $100–120) is less than a mile from downtown Franklin, near the Carter House. A large magnolia tree shades the early 20th-century Craftsman home. There are four carpeted guest rooms, each with a private bath. Three house queen-sized beds; the fourth has two twin beds. Common areas include a polished sitting room, cozy den, and sunroom that looks out on the quiet residential neighborhood. Hosts Jimmy and Robbie Smithson welcome guests and prepare homemade breakfast according to your preferences.

Also less than a mile from downtown, **Franklin House Bed and Breakfast** (304 Stewart St., 615/791-9895, www.bbonline.com/tn/franklinhouse, $125) has two queen-sized guest accommodations located upstairs in the 100-year-old farmhouse. Common areas include a gracious wraparound porch. Breakfast of homemade bread, breakfast casseroles, and other favorites is served in the spacious dining room.

❮ **Old Marshall House Bed and Breakfast** (1030 John Williams Rd., 615/791-1455, www.oldmarshallhouse.com, $120–170) is the best bed-and-breakfast in the Franklin area. The 19th-century farmhouse located about five miles east of the city has three bedrooms plus a unique log cabin on the grounds. King-sized guest rooms feature handmade quilts, large bathrooms, fireplaces, and private sitting areas. The queen-sized guest room, the most modestly priced, also has a private bathroom and

OUTSIDE NASHVILLE

its own cable TV and DVD player. Outside is a restored 1850s log cabin that has been carefully converted into a perfect overnight retreat. Guests enjoy a living room made cozy by a cast-iron gas stove, modern bathroom with a claw-foot tub, and king-sized sleeping loft. The cabin has a microwave, coffee-maker, and refrigerator and rents for $170 a night.

Weather permitting, breakfast is served on a terrace overlooking the five-acre yard. Dishes include French toast, fruit compote, and hash-brown quiche. The property is equipped with wireless Internet, and owners Glen and Ursula Houghton are friendly, knowledgeable, and seasoned hosts.

FOOD
Downtown

Think country buffet, and then think ten times better. **◖ Monell's** (108 Bridge St., 615/790-6993, Mon.–Fri. 10:30 A.M.–2 P.M., Tues.–Sat. 5–8:30 P.M., Sat. 8:30 A.M.–1 P.M., Sun. 8:30 A.M.–4 P.M., $13–20) does fine Southern cooking, served all-you-can-eat family style. Come in and you'll be seated at a long table with other diners. If you feel weird about that, well, get over it and just remember to pass the dishes to the left. Chances are you'll wind up enjoying the unexpected company. The tables at Monell's sag with good food. When you're seated you'll already find cold cucumber salad, coleslaw, and iced tea on the table. Soon after, the server will bring out plate after plate of more temptations: savory greens, fluffy biscuits, cheesy potato casserole, golden skillet-fried chicken, and much more. Each lunch or dinner they offer three different main-course meats, including things like chicken and dumplings, skillet-fried chicken, pot roast, pork chops, and meatloaf. The main dishes are accompanied by traditional country sides. Dessert may be banana pudding, fruit cobbler, or some other sweet specialty. For breakfast, expect smoked sausage, bacon, country ham, pancakes, hash browns, grits, and—if you can imagine it—more. Monell's is a great choice for those who love country cooking, for the uninitiated who want to try it out, and for all those in between.

The best choice for baked goods, coffee, and light fare, including soups, salads, and sandwiches, is **Merridee's Breadbasket** (110 4th Ave., 615/790-3755, Mon.–Sat. 7 A.M.–5 P.M., $3–7). Merridee grew up in Minnesota and learned baking from her mother, a Swede. When Merridee married Tom McCray and moved to Middle Tennessee in 1973, she kept up the baking traditions she had learned as a child. In 1984, she opened Merridee's Breadbasket in Franklin. Merridee McCray died in 1994, but her restaurant remains one of Franklin's most popular. Come in for omelets, scrambled eggs, or sweet bread and fruit in the morning. At lunch choose from the daily soup, casserole, or quiche, or order a cold or grilled sandwich. Merridee's also bakes fresh bread daily; take home a loaf of the always-popular Viking bread. Merridee's attracts a variety of people—students, businesspeople, and families out on the town. The creaky wood floors and comfortable seating make it a pleasant and relaxing place to refuel.

Puckett's Grocery and Restaurant (120 4th Ave. S., 615/794-5527), the Leiper's Fork institution, has expanded with a second location in Franklin. The Franklin shop offers traditional breakfasts with eggs, bacon, country ham, and biscuits and plate lunches in the day. In the evening, order up a handmade burger (the locals swear that they're the best in town), a Southern dinner of fried catfish, or traditional steak, chicken, or fish entrée. For vegetarians, they offer a veggie burger or a vegetable plate, as well as salads. The food is well prepared and the service friendly, and there's almost always a crowd.

Award-winning and always popular, **◖ Saffire** (The Factory, 615/599-4995, Tues.–Sun., $14–35) serves lunch 11 A.M.–3 P.M. and dinner beginning at 5 P.M. Using primarily organic and biodynamic ingredients, Saffire's menu sparkles with unique dishes. Try the tender and flavorful Cuban roasted pork appetizer plate, or a simple salad of heirloom tomatoes. Entrées include upscale dishes like prime rib and ahi tuna. Their fried chicken is dusted with Panko flakes, topped with country ham gravy, and served with luscious macaroni and cheese. Saffire has an extensive wine and cocktail list, including organic choices. Take $4 off signature cocktails during happy hour (5–6 P.M.) and on Tuesday night most bottles of wine go for half-price. The lunch menu is casual, featuring sandwiches, salads, and lunch-sized entrées. Or choose the "green plate" daily special, featuring local and organic ingredients. There is also a midday kid's menu with favorites like grilled cheese and chicken bites.

Set within an old warehouse, Saffire's dining room is spacious with exposed brick and beams. The kitchen opens out onto the dining room, so you can watch the cooks work. With live music many nights, Saffire is a fine choice for excellent food in a pleasant and exciting environment.

Farmer's Market

The Franklin Farmer's Market takes place at the rear of the Factory on Saturday mornings during spring, summer, and fall 8 A.M.–noon. This is one of the finest small-town farmer's markets in the state, featuring a wide variety of fruit and vegetable growers, and cheese, milk, and meat sellers, as well as craftspersons and live music.

INFORMATION

The **Williamson County Convention and Visitors Bureau** (615/791-7554 or 866/253-9207, www.visitwilliamson.com) publishes guides and maintains a website about Franklin and the surrounding area. They also operate the **Williamson County Visitor Center** (209 E. Main St., 615/591-8514, Mon.–Fri. 9 A.M.–4 P.M., Sat. 10 A.M.–3 P.M., Sun. noon–3 P.M.).

Walking Horse Country

The territory directly south of Nashville is Tennessee Walking Horse Country. The high-stepping, smooth-riding Tennessee Walking Horse is bred on horse farms that dot the landscape.

The attractions are more than horses, however. The town of Bell Buckle is a charming pit stop for country cooking and antiques shopping and Wartrace has a lovely old-fashioned railroad hotel. For the best distillery tour in Tennessee, head to the George Dickel Distillery near Normandy; for the most popular, press on to Lynchburg and the Jack Daniel's Distillery.

BELL BUCKLE

A tiny town nestled in the northern reaches of the Walking Horse region, Bell Buckle is a charming place to visit. Once a railroad town, Bell Buckle has successfully become a destination for antiques shopping, arts and crafts, small-town hospitality, and country cooking. The town's single commercial street faces the old railroad tracks; handsome old homes—some

of them bed-and-breakfast inns—spread out along quiet residential streets.

What makes Bell Buckle so appealing is the sense of humor that permeates just about everything that happens here. T-shirts for sale on the main street proclaim "Tokyo, Paris, New York, Bell Buckle," and the town's quirky residents feel free to be themselves. Tennessee's poet laureate, Margaret "Maggie" Britton Vaughn, who operates the Bell Buckle Press and had an office on Main Street for many years, once told an interviewer that William Faulkner "would have killed" for a community with the ambience and characters, of Bell Buckle.

Bell Buckle's name is derived from the Bell Buckle Creek, named thus because a cow's bell was found hanging in a tree by the creek, attached by a buckle.

The town's annual Moon Pie Festival in June attracts thousands to the small town, and the Webb School Arts and Crafts Festival in October is one of the finest regional arts shows in the state.

Sights

Bell Buckle is noted as the home of the elite and well-regarded **Webb School.** Founded in 1870 and led by William Robert Webb until his death in 1926, Webb School has graduated 10 Rhodes scholars, several governors, attorneys general, and numerous successful academics. The school now has about 300 students in grades 8 through 12 from around the country and the world. While it was all-male for many years of its life, Webb School now admits both male and female students. Its athletic mascot is the "Webb Feet."

The Webb campus is about three blocks north of downtown Bell Buckle. You can visit the main administrative office during regular business hours, where there are photographs and school memorabilia on display.

Events

Bell Buckle's biggest annual event is the **RC and Moon Pie Festival** in mid-June. This weekend event includes country and bluegrass music, Moon Pie games, arts and crafts booths, the crowning of a Moon Pie King and Queen, and a 10-mile run. You can also witness the cutting of the world's largest Moon Pie. In case you're wondering why Bell Buckle has rights to the Moon Pie festival, it's because they asked for it.

The **Webb School Arts and Crafts Festival** brings hundreds of artisans to town. It is one of the finest arts and crafts shows in the region, attracting fine and folk artists from Tennessee and beyond.

Shopping

The single most popular pursuit in Bell Buckle is shopping. Antiques are the main attraction, but arts and crafts are a close second.

The **Bell Buckle Art Gallery** (26 Railroad Sq., 931/389-0004) sells a wide selection of artwork, from pottery and sculpture to paintings. Most pieces here have a fresh, modern appeal.

The Cat's Meow (25 Railroad Sq., 931/389-0064) has purses, totes, linens, throws, and jewelry, plus lots of gifts for babies and new

antique shopping in Bell Buckle

PHOTO COURTESY THE TENNESSEE DEPARTMENT OF TOURIST DEVELOPMENT

parents. The **Doodle Bug** and **Doodle Bug Too** (Railroad Sq., 931/389-9009) are sister shops that sell jewelry, housewares, gifts, and folk art.

For antiques try the **Bell Buckle Antique Mall** (112 Main St., 931/389-6174) or **Blue Ribbon Antiques** (Railroad Sq., 931/684-2588).

Accommodations

Hostess Ina Mingle runs the **Mingle House Bed and Breakfast** (116 Main St., 931/389-9453, $80–85) in a restored 1898 Victorian home. Rooms are furnished with antiques, and guests can fuel up with a country-style breakfast of eggs, sausage, bacon, and more in the morning.

Food

There's no debate about where to eat in Bell Buckle. The 【 **Bell Buckle Cafe** (Railroad Sq., 931/389-9693, Mon. 10:30 A.M.–2 P.M., Tues.–Thurs. 10:30 A.M.–8 P.M., Fri.–Sat. 10:30 A.M.–9 P.M., Sun. 11 A.M.–5 P.M., $5–15)

THE TENNESSEE WALKING HORSE

Considered the world's greatest pleasure, trail, and show horse, the Tennessee Walking Horse is the first breed of horse to bear the name of a state. Tennessee Walkers existed for many years before the breed was identified and named; early settlers needed horses that could travel easily and comfortably over rocky and uneven terrain. These early walkers were not trained to show – they were purely utilitarian.

In 1886 a black colt named Black Allan was foaled. He was the result of a cross between a stallion called Allendorf, from the Hambletonian family of trotters, and Maggie Marshall, a Morgan mare. Black Allen was crossed with a Tennessee Pacer, and the modern Tennessee Walking Horse breed was born.

Tennessee Walkers are known for their docile temperament and kind manner. They are also known for their unique running walk –

The Tennessee Walking Horse is a champion show horse.

in which each of the horse's hooves hit the ground separately at regular intervals. In this gait, the animal's front legs rise in an exaggerated step and the horse's head nods in time with the rhythm of its legs.

PHOTO COURTESY OF THE TENN DEPT OF TOURIST DEVELOPMENT

is not only a Bell Buckle institution, it's the only game in town. The menu is Southern, with a few refined touches (like ostrich burger and spinach-strawberry salad) you won't find at most small-town cafés. The menu is also mighty diverse, with seafood, pasta, and sandwiches in addition to the usual plate lunches and dinner entrées. The large dining room fills up quick, especially for lunch, so there's no shame in coming a bit early. The Bell Buckle Cafe takes care of your entertainment needs too. There's always live music on Thursday, Friday, and Saturday night, usually bluegrass or country. Local radio station WLIJ broadcasts a musical variety show from the café on Saturday 1–3 P.M., which is a great reason to come to the café for lunch.

If you managed to pass up homemade dessert at the Bell Buckle Cafe, then head to **Bluebird Antiques and Ice Cream Parlor** (15 Webb Rd., 931/389-6549). Here you'll find a turn-of-the-20th-century soda fountain with hand-dipped ice cream and homemade waffle cones. Come in the morning to see (and smell) them making the cones. Not to be missed.

Information

The **Bell Buckle Chamber of Commerce** (931/389-9663, www.bellbucklechamber.com) publishes brochures, promotes the town, and operates as a clearinghouse for information.

WARTRACE

This tiny railroad town about 10 miles east of Shelbyville is the birthplace of the Tennessee Walking Horse. It was on the grounds of the town's Walking Horse Hotel that Albert Dement trained a $350 plow horse into **Strolling Jim,** the first world grand champion walking horse. Strolling Jim died in 1957; you can visit his grave in the pasture behind the hotel, across the railroad tracks from the town square.

The annual walking horse celebration that now draws a quarter million people to Shelbyville every year started in Wartrace, but got too big for the small town and moved to Shelbyville in 1935.

Accommodations

The ◖ **Walking Horse Hotel** (101 Spring St.,

BONNAROO

Bonnaroo Music and Arts Festival (www. bonnaroo.com) started out in 2002 as a jam band music festival, but diversification has made this summertime mega event a destination for all types of music fans. The 'Roo takes place over four days in June on a rural farm in Manchester. Between 75,000 and 90,000 people come each year.

Bonnaroo has a hippie heart with a slightly hard edge. Place names are Suessian – the music tents are called, from largest to small-

est, What Stage, Which Stage, This Tent, That Tent, and The Other Tent. Activities run the gamut from a Mardi Gras parade to kid's art activities. Of course, it's the music that really draws the crowds: reggae, rock, Americana, jam bands, world, hip-hop, jazz, electronic, folk, gospel, and country. The event is truly a feast for the ears.

In 2007, the Police were reunited at Bonnaroo. In 2008, headliners included Kanye West, Willie Nelson, and Pearl Jam. But quality

PHOTO COURTESY OF THE TENN DEPT OF TOURIST DEVELOPMENT

Bonnaroo Music and Arts Festival

931/389-7030, www.walkinghorsehotel.com) is the best place to stay not only in Wartrace, but for a good distance in any direction. When Joe Peters bought the hotel in 2007 he was intent on paying tribute to his late wife, Chais, who loved the old 1917 hotel. Peters and his family have brought new life to the old hotel by refurbishing the rooms, recruiting beloved chef Bill Hall to run the Strolling Jim Restaurant, and opening the Chais Music Hall, a state-of-the-art venue for all types of music.

Rooms are a fusion of old and new. Classic touches from the hotel's early days have been preserved, but guests can expect the best modern amenities, including flat-screen

televisions, wireless Internet, super-comfortable beds, and good linens.

Another choice in Wartrace is the **Historic Main Street Inn** (207 Main St. E., 931/389-0389, www.historicmainstreetinn.com, $95–115), a bed-and-breakfast located half a block from main street. Each of the five guest rooms are lavishly decorated in a romantic style fitting for the 1906 Queen Anne home. All rooms have a private bath—some have antique claw-footed tubs. Breakfast here is nothing simple or quick; expect choices like homemade fruit crepes, baked apple pancake, or stuffed French toast. Built by a local banker, the home has been operated as a bed-and-breakfast since 1996.

permeates every echelon of the stage. Unknowns and barely-knowns routinely wow audiences. There is a big emphasis on world artists and folk music. A jazz tent provides nightclub ambience, and there's even a comedy tent.

A few things to know about Bonnaroo: First, it's huge. The event takes place on a 700-acre farm, and the list of offerings is seemingly endless: four stages of music, whole villages dedicated to the arts, a 24-hour movie tent, yoga studio, salon, children's activity tents, music-industry showcase, food vendors, and a whole lot more.

Second, Bonnaroo has above-average logistics. Organizers seem to consider everything, including the basics: drinking water, medical care, parking, traffic control, and a general store where you can buy necessities. Food vendors sell Tennessee barbecue, veggie burgers, and just about everything in between. A shuttle service between the Nashville airport and the 'Roo helps minimize traffic. Rules about camping, RVs, re-entry, and security are common-sense and easy to follow.

All that said, you can't turn up with the clothes on your back and expect to have much fun. It's important to pack well: A good camping tent, folding chairs, and water bottles are important. Even if you plan to buy most of your food,

at least pack some snacks. There are ATMs at the 'Roo, but lines can be very long, so bringing plenty of cash is also a good idea (but not too much, since you don't want to attract trouble). Also bring garbage bags, sunscreen, and hot-weather, comfortable clothes. Rain renders the farm to mud, so if the weather is iffy – or even if it's not – pack sturdy shoes and a rain coat.

Plenty of Bonnaroo fans take the opportunity to do a lot of drinking and drugs. There are police at the festival, but they don't seem to crack down on every recreational drug user. Beer – including good microbrews – are sold, and consumed generously. That said, getting wasted is not everyone's idea of a good time and if you decide to stay sober, you'll be in good company.

Most people buy a four-day pass to the festival, but day-pass tickets are available too. Four-day passes cost $200 and up; a limited number of reduced-price early-bird tickets go on sale in January each year. Regular tickets go on sale in the spring, after the line-up has been announced.

In 2007, Bonnaroo producers bought most of the farm where the festival is held, saying that they want to improve water lines and roads. They may also start hosting smaller events there during the year.

Food

The **Iron Gait** (106 Fairfield Rd., 931/389-6001, Mon.–Fri. 7 A.M.–2 P.M., Sat. 7 A.M.–7 P.M., Sun. 1–4 P.M., $3–8) serves breakfast, burgers, and meat-and-three dinners. The monster burger is a favorite, as are the plate lunches. Find the Iron Gait just around the corner from Main Street, on the road to Bell Buckle.

For other dining choices, look in Bell Buckle, Normandy, and Shelbyville.

Information

The **Wartrace Chamber of Commerce** (931/389-9999, www.wartracechamber.com) promotes the town.

NORMANDY

Normandy is a tiny one-street town, notable for its position on the railroad and its location amid some of the most beautiful countryside in this part of Tennessee. The rural routes surrounding Normandy are well worth exploring.

◖ George Dickel Distillery

About seven miles south of Wartrace, just outside of the old railroad town of Normandy, is one of the best-kept secrets in this part of Tennessee. The George Dickel Distillery (931/857-3124, Tues.–Sat. 9 A.M.–4 P.M.) makes thousands of gallons of Tennessee sipping whisky every year, and all of it comes from the Dickel distillery

VANNOY STREETER

Self-taught folk artist Vannoy Streeter drew inspiration for his work from the elegant stride and unique step of the Tennessee Walking Horse. Born in Wartrace in 1919 and raised on a horse farm, Streeter first displayed his remarkable talent as a child. His family could not afford to buy toy airplanes and cars, so he made them – bending them out of bailing wire.

Streeter was in Wartrace for the first Walking Horse Celebration, and in later years he returned to the event after it moved to Shelbyville. Streeter was proud of the fact that African Americans trained Strolling Jim and many other world-champion walking horses. He created hundreds, if not thousands, of sculpted horses, each with the distinctive high-stepping front leg and each with an African-American rider on the back. Other favorite subjects were performers – he sculpted Tina Turner and Elvis Presley in particular – and vehicles, including big-rig trucks, locomotives, and airplanes.

Streeter made most of his sculptures out of coat-hanger wire; he bought hangers by the hundreds. He did detail work with fine-gauge wire and large-scale work with bracing wire. He worked with regular pliers, wire cutters, and needle-nosed pliers.

Streeter worked on the railroads, and as a lumberyard hand, janitor, and hospital orderly. In 1960 he met and married his wife, Marie, and became father to her six children. He continued to make his wire sculptures, eventually gaining national attention. In 1990 he was a demonstrating artist at the National Black Arts Festival in Atlanta and in 1992 Shelbyville proclaimed Vannoy Streeter Day. His work has been displayed in the White House and at the Tennessee State Museum in Nashville.

Streeter continued to work until his death in 1998, although his productivity declined after his wife's death. His work is sold in folk art galleries in Nashville and other cities, and has been included in African-American and folk art exhibits in Tennessee and elsewhere.

up Cascade Hollow on the Highland Rim of the Cumberland Plateau. (In deference to its connection to scotch, Dickel uses the Scottish spelling for whisky, without the "e.")

It's no secret that the best-known name in whiskey is distilled a few miles down the road in Lynchburg, but the folks at George Dickel don't seem to mind. The Dickel distillery is a smaller operation, and visitors are given a more personalized and detailed look at the operations of the plant. And the setting in the Cascade Hollow is one of the most charming in this part of the state.

George Dickel, a German immigrant, distilled his first bottle of whisky at Cascade Hollow in 1870. Dickel created a unique cold mellowing process, which made his product smoother than others. The distillery still uses Dickel's cold mellowing process, as well as his signature proportions of corn, malt, and rye. The Dickel distillery closed down during Prohibition, only to reopen in the 1950s.

The distillery has changed hands several times over the past 50 years, and it is now owned by Diageo, one of the largest beer, wine, and spirits manufacturers in the world.

Visitors can get a free one-hour tour of the distillery, which takes you through every step in the process. The last tour departs at 3:30 P.M.

To find George Dickel, take Route 269 to Normandy, where you will see signs pointing you to Cascade Hollow Road.

Accommodations

For a high-class country escape, head to the **❰ Parish Patch Farm and Inn** (1100 Cortner Rd., 931/857-3017, www.parishpatch.com, $80–220), an inn, conference center, and restaurant set in the rural countryside near Normandy. The more than 30 guest rooms are scattered in various buildings on this working farm. They include spacious suites, private cottages, standard-sized bedrooms, and rustic rooms in an old gristmill. The two least expensive rooms share a bath; all other rooms have private bathrooms, televisions, and telephones. Rollaway beds are available. All guests can enjoy the full country breakfast served daily in the inn dining room. Other amenities include a swimming pool, walking trails, a book and video library, hammocks, and lots of countryside to explore. Parish Patch is a working farm, so you can also watch (or join in) on farm chores, pick your own blackberries (in season, of course) or just watch the animals. The Duck River flows through the property, providing opportunities for fishing or canoeing.

Food

The **Cortner Mill Restaurant** (1100 Cortner Rd., 931/857-3018, www.parishpatch.com, Tues.–Sat. 5:30–9 P.M., $16–42) is an upscale country restaurant that serves dinner five nights a week and is often booked for special events. Specialties include Memphis-style dry-rub barbecue ribs, grilled rack of lamb, baked rainbow trout, and frog legs. There is an extensive wine list, and desserts include a flaming bananas foster made tableside. The restaurant hosts special buffets on Easter, Thanksgiving, Christmas, and New Year's Day, and the Champagne Sunday Brunch (Sun. 11:30 A.M.–1:30 P.M.) is a popular treat for locals and visitors.

The restaurant is located in a restored 1825 gristmill and the dining room overlooks the river. It is an elegant choice for a special dinner.

LYNCHBURG

Lynchburg, no longer population 361, has been transformed by the popularity of Jack Daniel's Tennessee Whiskey, which is made a few blocks from the town square. No other small town in Tennessee sees as many visitors, from as many different places, as this one.

Critics may object to the tour buses and crowds, but for now, the town has managed to survive its success with relative grace. It has maintained its small-town feel, and it offers its guests a hospitable and heartfelt welcome.

Lynchburg is centered around the Moore County courthouse, a modest redbrick building. Souvenir shops, restaurants, and a few local businesses line the square. Outside of this, Lynchburg is quiet and residential. The Jack Daniel's Distillery is about three blocks away from the town square; a pleasant footpath connects the two.

Jack Daniel's Distillery

As you drive into Lynchburg, or walk around the town, you might notice some odd-looking grey warehouses peeking out above the treetops. These are barrel houses, where Jack Daniel's Distillery ages its whiskey. Around Moore County there are 74 of these warehouses, and each one holds about one million barrels of whiskey.

Thousands of whiskey drinkers make the pilgrimage every year to Jack Daniel's Distillery (280 Lynchburg Hwy., aka Hwy. 55, 931/759-4221, www.jackdaniels.com, daily 9 A.M.–4:30 P.M., free) to see how Jack Daniel's is made. And what they find is that, aside from

the Lynchburg town square

© SUSANNA HENIGHAN POTTER

the use of electricity, computers, and the sheer scale of the operation, things have not changed too much since 1866 when Jack Daniel registered his whiskey still at the mouth of Cave Spring near Lynchburg.

Jack Daniel was an interesting man. He stood just 5 feet, 2 inches tall and liked to wear three-piece suits. He was introduced to the whiskey business by a Lutheran lay preacher named Dan Call, who sold the distillery to Daniel shortly after the Civil War. In 1866, Daniel had the foresight to register his distillery with the federal government, making his the oldest registered distillery in the United States. He never married and had no known children.

Daniel died of gangrene in 1911. He got it from kicking a metal safe in frustration after he couldn't get it open, and breaking his toe. After Daniel died, the distillery passed to his nephew, Lem Motlow. The distillery remained in the Motlow family until it was sold in 1957 to the Brown-Forman Corporation of Louisville, Kentucky.

The one-hour tour of the distillery begins with a video about the master distillers—Jack Daniel's has had seven in its lifetime—who are the final authority on all facets of the product. You then board a bus that takes you up to the far side of the distillery, and from here you'll walk back to the visitors center, stopping frequently to be told about the key steps in the process. The highlight of the tour for some is seeing Cave Spring, where the distillery gets its iron-free spring water. Others enjoy taking a potent whiff of the sour mash and the mellowing whiskey.

The tour ends back at the visitors center where you are served free lemonade and coffee. Moore County, where Lynchburg is located, is a dry county and for 86 years the irony was that Jack Daniel's could not sell any of its whiskey at the distillery. In 1995, however, the county approved a special exemption that allows the distillery to sell souvenir bottles of whiskey at its visitors center. That is all they sell, however; you have to buy other Jack Daniel's merchandise at one of the gift shops in town.

A statue of Jack Daniel stands sentry in front of Cave Spring at the Jack Daniel's Distillery.

Other Sights

A stately two-story brick building on the southwest corner of the square is the **Moore County Jail** (231 Main St., mid-Mar.–Dec. Tues.–Sat. 11 A.M.–3 P.M., free), which served as the sheriff's residence and the county jail until 1990. The building is now a museum and is operated by the local historical society. You can see law-enforcement memorabilia, old newspaper clippings, and vintage clothes. Go upstairs to see the prisoners' cells.

Just down Main Street is the **Tennessee Walking Horse Museum** (Public Sq., 931/759-5747, Tues.–Sat. 9 A.M.–5 P.M., free). The museum was originally located in Shelbyville, but moved to Lynchburg in the early 2000s to take advantage of the bustling tourist trade here.

The Walking Horse Museum displays photographs, trophies, and other memorabilia from walking horse champions. You can admire both show and posed photographs of top horses, and watch a video that explains what makes the walking horse so special. The films include show footage of the breed's distinctive flat walk, fast walk, and canter.

Accommodations

The **Lynchburg Bed and Breakfast** (Mechanic St., 931/759-7158, www.bbonline.com/tn/lynchburg, $70) has been welcoming guests to Lynchburg since 1985. There are two guest rooms; one has a queen-sized bed and one has two twin beds. Each room has a private bathroom and cable TV; a shared telephone and refrigerator are in the hallway between the two rooms. Guests are served a continental breakfast. Accommodations are homey, but not luxurious.

The **Tolley House** (1253 Main St., 931/759-7263, www.tolleyhouse.com, $135–150) is located about a mile from the town square, and is a pleasant country retreat. A handsome antebellum farmhouse once owned by Jack Daniel's master distiller Lem Motlow, the Tolley House provides touches of luxury. Rooms have private baths, television, and wireless Internet access, and are furnished tastefully with antiques. Hosts Frank and Karen Fletcher provide your

choice of a full country or light continental breakfast. Discounts are available for stays of two or more nights.

The closest thing to a motel in Lynchburg is the **Lynchburg Country Inn** (423 Majors Blvd., 931/759-5995, www.lynchburgcountryinn.com, $55–65). Its 25 rooms are each furnished with a microwave, refrigerator, and cable TV. There's a pool out back and rocking chairs on the front and back porches. The building is modern, built in 2003, but the decor is pure country.

Food

The most popular place to eat in Lynchburg is **❰ Miss Mary Bobo's Boarding House** (295 Main St., 931/759-7394, Mon.–Sat. lunch only, $19). Miss Mary's started life as the home of Thomas Roundtree, the founder of Lynchburg. It later became the home of Dr. E. Y. Salmon, a Confederate captain, who maintained an office there and rented out rooms to boarders. In 1908, Lacy Jackson Bobo and his wife, Mary Evans Bobo, bought the house and continued to operate it as a boarding house until the 1980s. Over the years, word of Mary Bobo's legendary home-cooked meals spread and this boarding house became one of the region's best-known eating houses. Today, Miss Mary's is no longer a boarding house, and the restaurant is operated by Miss Lynne Tolley, who has worked hard to keep up the traditions established by Miss Mary. The restaurant is owned by the Jack Daniel's Distillery, and servers are hired from the local community college. A meal at Miss Mary's will easily be the most unique of your trip. On most days there are two seatings—11 A.M. and 1 P.M. Guests should arrive at least 15 minutes early so you can check in, pay, and be assigned to a dining room. When the dinner bell rings, you will be taken to your dining room by a hostess, who stays with you throughout the meal. Everyone sits family-style around a big table. The meal served at Miss Mary's is a traditional Southern dinner. You'll find no less than six side dishes and two meats, plus iced tea (unsweetened), dessert, coffee, and bread. Almost every meal features fried chicken. Side dishes may include green beans, mashed potatoes, fried okra, carrot slaw, and corn bread. Your hostess will make sure that everyone has enough to eat, answer questions about the food, and tell you some stories about the restaurant—if you ask. Be sure to call well ahead to make your reservations. Meals are fully booked weeks and even months in advance, especially during the busy summer months and on Saturdays.

For a more low-key meal, go to the **Bar-B-Que Caboose Cafe** (217 Main St., 931/759-5180, daily 11 A.M.–5 P.M., $7–12). The menu offers pulled-pork barbecue sandwiches, jambalaya,

red beans and rice, and hot dogs. You can also get pizzas. On Friday night (April–October) the restaurant opens for dinner 6:30–8 P.M. and you can get a barbecue plate dinner for $9 while you listen to live music. On Saturday morning from 10 to 11 A.M. a live country music radio show is broadcast from the Caboose Cafe.

There are a handful of other restaurants in Lynchburg, all on the town square. **Elk Coffee** (12 Short St., 931/759-5552, Mon.–Sat. 8 A.M.–5:30 P.M., Sun. noon–5 P.M., $6–12) sells lighter fare, including wraps and salads.

Be forewarned that it is next to impossible to get an evening meal in Lynchburg. By 6 P.M. the place is a ghost town.

The Natchez Trace

The Natchez Trace Parkway cuts a diagonal path through the heartland south of Nashville. The two-lane limited-access highway passes through mostly undeveloped countryside.

Simply driving the Trace is pleasant enough, but short detours to villages and county seats along the way make this a lovely getaway that balances quiet exploration with sights and attractions.

LEIPER'S FORK

Part small town, part yuppified enclave, Leiper's Fork is a pleasant place to spend a few hours. It is located about 15 minutes' drive from Franklin and near milepost 420 on the Natchez Trace Parkway.

Leiper's Fork is a pleasant community. Art galleries and antiques shops line the short main drag. Unusually good food can be found at local restaurants and a laid-back let's-laugh-at-ourselves attitude prevails.

Shopping

Leiper's Fork retailers are open Wednesday–Saturday 10 A.M.–5 P.M. and Sunday 1–5 P.M.

Opening its doors in 2007, **R Place** (4154 Old Hillsboro Rd.) sells the artwork of Anne Goetz, the handmade furniture of Reed Birnie,

and used books curated by Renee Armand. You can also get homemade pie and coffee if you need sustenance while you browse the shop, housed in an old home.

The **Leiper's Creek Gallery** (4144 Old Hillsboro Rd., 615/599-5102) is the finest gallery in town. It shows a wide selection of paintings by local and regional artists and hosts a variety of arts events year-round.

Neena's Primitive Antiques (4158 Old Hillsboro Rd., 615/790-0345) specializes in primitive antiques, linens, home decor items, and leather goods.

Entertainment

Friday night is songwriter night at **Puckett's Grocery** (4142 Old Hillsboro Rd., 615/794-1308, www.puckettsgrocery.com). For $30 you enjoy dressed-up dinner—fresh seafood, poultry, and steak are usually among the options—at 7 P.M. and an in-the-round performance from Nashville singer-songwriters starting at 8:30 P.M. If you prefer, pay $15 for the concert only. Reservations are essential for either, so call ahead. Check the website to find out who is performing.

Jailhouse Industries operates the Leiper's Fork **Lawn Chair Theatre** from May to

driving along the Natchez Trace Parkway

September. Bring your lawn chair or blanket and enjoy classic movies and kids' favorites on Friday and Saturday nights. Call 615/477-6799 for more information, or just ask around.

Hiking

The Leiper's Fork District of the Natchez Trace National Scenic Trail runs for 24 miles, starting near milepost 427 and ending at milepost 408, where State Highway 50 crosses the parkway. The trail follows the old Natchez Trace through rural countryside.

The best access point is from Garrison Creek Road, where there is parking, restrooms, and picnic facilities. You can also access the trail from Davis Hollow Road.

Accommodations

Namaste Acres (5436 Leiper's Creek Rd., 615/791-0333, www.bbonline.com/tn/namaste, $120–175) is a unique bed-and-breakfast. Located on a working horse farm, Namaste Acres guests are treated to beautiful farm views and hearty country breakfasts. Three guest suites are decorated with a Western flair: lots of exposed wood, rocking chairs, and woven Indian rugs. Horse owners can board their horses here too. Each suite has a private bathroom, deck, and fireplace, as well as a TV/VCR, telephone, refrigerator, and coffee-maker.

Food

◖ Puckett's Grocery (4142 Old Hillsboro Rd., 615/794-1308, www.puckettsgrocery. com, daily 6 A.M.–6 P.M., $6–25) is home to the heartbeat of Leiper's Fork. An old-time grocery with a small dining room attached, Puckett's serves breakfast, lunch, and dinner to the town faithful and visitors alike. The original country store opened about 1950. In 1998, Andy Marshall bought the store and expanded the restaurant offerings. Solid country breakfasts are the order of the day in the mornings, followed by plate lunches. The pulled pork is a favorite, as is the Puckett Burger. Dinner specials include catfish nights, family nights, and a Saturday-night seafood buffet. Friday night the grocery turns upscale with a supper club and live music. Reservations are essential for Friday night. Puckett's hours vary by the season, so it is best to call ahead, especially for dinner arrangements. A second Puckett's Grocery location in Franklin offers a more varied menu.

For a casual sandwich, decadent pastry, or cup of coffee, head to the **Backyard Cafe** (4150 Old Hillsboro Rd., 615/790-4003, Mon.–Sat. 11 A.M.–3 P.M., Sun. noon–3 P.M.).

THE NATCHEZ TRACE

The first people to travel what is now regarded as the Natchez Trace were probably Choctow and Chickasaw Indians, who made the first footpaths through the region. French and Spanish traders used the 500 miles of intertwining Indian trails that linked the Mississippi port of Natchez to the Cumberland River.

Early white settlers quickly identified the importance of a land route from Natchez to Nashville. In 1801, the Natchez Trace opened as an official post road between the two cities. Boatmen who piloted flatboats from Nashville and other northern cities to Natchez and New Orleans returned along the Trace by foot or horse, often carrying large sums of money. One historian characterized the diverse array of people who used the Trace: "robbers, rugged pioneers, fashionable ladies, shysters, politicians, soldiers, scientists, and men of destiny, such as Aaron Burr, Andrew Jackson and Meriwether Lewis."

The Trace developed a reputation for robberies, and few people traveled its miles alone. Many thieves disguised themselves as Indians, fanning the flames of racial distrust that existed during this period of history. By 1820, more than 20 inns, referred to as "stands," were open. Many were modest – providing food and shelter only.

In 1812, the first steamship arrived at Natchez, Mississippi, marking the beginning of the end of the Trace's prominence. As steamboat

The bridge at milepost 438 along the Natchez Trace Parkway is an architectural marvel.

travel became more widespread and affordable, more and more people turned away from the long, laborious, and dangerous overland route along the Trace.

Information

The **Leiper's Fork Merchant's Association** (615/972-2708, www.leipersforkvillage.com) promotes the town, maintains a listing of local businesses, and publishes an annual calendar of events.

SPRING HILL

A small town midway between Franklin and Columbia, Spring Hill is best known by many as the site of a large General Motors automobile factory. To students of

the Civil War, the town is the site of one of the South's greatest missed opportunities of the war. While it is doubtful that a different outcome at Spring Hill would have changed the course of war, it would very likely have saved the many thousands of lives lost at the Battle of Franklin.

Spring Hill is located along U.S. Highway 31. Downtown consists of a few blocks between Beechcroft and Kendron Roads. The town's main street was destroyed by fire and tornado in 1963, leaving only a few remnants

The road's historical importance is evident in the fact that it was not easily forgotten. While it faded from use, the Natchez Trace was remembered. In 1909, the Daughters of the American Revolution in Mississippi started a project to mark the route of the Trace in each county through which it passed. The marker project continued for the next 24 years and eventually caught the attention of Mississippi Rep. Thomas J. Busby, who introduced the first bills in Congress to survey and construct a paved road along the route of the old Natchez Trace.

During the Great Depression, work on the Natchez Trace Parkway began under the Public Works Administration, the Works Project Administration, and the Civilian Conservation Corps. Following the New Deal, construction slowed dramatically and it was not until 1996 that the final leg of the parkway was completed.

The 445-mile parkway follows the general path of the old Natchez Trace; in a few places, they fall in step with each other. Just over 100 miles of the parkway lie within Tennessee. It runs along the Western Highland Rim through Davidson, Williamson, Hickman, Maury, Lewis, and Wayne Counties.

The parkway passes scenic overlooks, historic sites, and quiet pastures. In many places along the route you have the opportunity to walk along the original Trace.

ACCOMMODATIONS AND FOOD
There are no hotels on the parkway. Look for accommodations in nearby cities, including Franklin, Columbia, and Lawrenceburg. The Hampshire-based **Natchez Trace Reservation Service** (800/377-2770, www.bbonline.com/natcheztrace) books bed-and-breakfast inns along the parkway, from Nashville all the way to Natchez. This service is worth considering, especially since many of these inns are located closer to the parkway than motels are.

The closest accommodations to the parkway are three **campgrounds,** one of which lies in Tennessee. The Meriwether Lewis Campground at milepost 385 has 32 sites and a bathhouse. The next campground is Jeff Busby at milepost 193, in Mississippi.

There are no restaurants or food concessions along the parkway. Picnic facilities abound, however, so wise travelers will pack a few sandwiches and avoid traveling off the parkway to eat.

INFORMATION AND SERVICES
The **National Park Service** (800/305-7417, www.nps.gov/natr) publishes a fold-out map and guide to the parkway. The official visitors center for the parkway is in Tupelo, Mississippi. For detailed hiking information, visit the website about the Natchez Trace National Scenic Trail at www.nps.gov/natt.

The only gas station along the parkway is at Jeff Busby, milepost 193, in Mississippi. Fill up your tank before you take off to explore.

OUTSIDE NASHVILLE

of Spring Hill's former charm. To see them, drive up and down the town's side streets, including Murray Hill, Depot, and McLemore Streets. Spring Hill's main attractions are along Highway 31 less than a mile outside of town.

The **Spring Hill Battlefield** (931/486-9037) is a 118-acre park with a one-mile trail that climbs to the top of a hill overlooking the battlefield. Interpretive markers tell the story of Spring Hill. The park is open during daylight hours. To find it, turn east onto Kendron Road and look for the park on the right-hand side of the road, just before the road passes I-65.

Rippavilla
You can tour an 1850s-era mansion at Rippavilla Plantation (5700 Main St., aka Hwy. 31, 931/486-9037, www.rippavilla.org, Tues.–Sat. 9 A.M.–5 P.M., adults $8, seniors $6, children 6–12 $5, children under 6 free), just south of downtown Spring Hill on Highway 31. Rippavilla, originally called Rip-o-villa,

OUTSIDE NASHVILLE

THE FARM

In 1970, hippie spiritual leader Stephen Gaskin and 320 others established a commune in the rural Tennessee countryside near Summertown, Tennessee. Initially governed by beliefs that forbade alcohol and birth control and promoted nonviolence and respect for the environment, the Farm has evolved over the years. While it has loosened some rules, it remains committed to peace, justice, and environmental sustainability.

The Farm has established a number of successful businesses, and it has contributed to its mission for a more peaceful and healthy world. Its businesses include a book publishing company, a soy dairy that manufactures tofu and soy milk, and a yoga studio. Farm books include *The Farm Vegetarian Cookbook* and Ina May Gaskin's works on natural childbirth. Nonprofits on the Farm include Plenty International, an international aid organization, and the Farm School, which provides alternative education for primary through secondary grades.

The Farm is glad to receive visitors. The Ecovillage Training Center puts on workshops and conferences throughout the year, many of them dealing with organic gardening, permaculture, construction, and other sustainable technologies. The Farm also operates a midwifery training center and birthing houses, where women can come to give birth.

About 200 people live at the Farm today. A few have been there since the beginning, but there are also recent transplants. Some work at Farm enterprises, but others have jobs "off the Farm." Farm members become shareholders in the company that owns the Farm land and other assets.

VISITING THE FARM

The Farm is a welcoming and friendly place, where people wave at each other and you can strike up a conversation with just about anybody. The **Welcome Center** (100 Farm Rd., 931/964-3574, www.thefarmcommunity.com) has a museum about the community and sells Farm books, T-shirts, and other products. It is usually open Monday-Friday 1-5 P.M., but it is a good idea to call ahead to confirm; hours are normally cut back from November to March. You can arrange for a tour with a member of the Farm by calling ahead to the welcome center. There are also twice-yearly Farm Experience weekends for people who want to see what Farm living is about.

The **Farm Store** (931/964-4356) is open daily 9 A.M.-7 P.M. and sells organic and natural groceries, household items, vegetarian sandwiches, and drinks.

ACCOMMODATIONS

You can sleep the night at the Farm. The Inn at the Farm is part of the EcoVillage Training Center, and it offers dormitory-style accommodations. Reservations are required, and the inn is sometimes full when there are workshops or conferences underway.

A half-dozen farm residents rent out rooms to visitors, usually for about $35 a night per person. Meals may be available for an additional fee. There is also a campground, where you can pitch your own tent. For more information about staying at the Farm, call the welcome center or go online.

GETTING THERE

The Farm is located off Drake's Lane Road, a few miles west of Summertown along Route 20. Detailed directions and a map are available on the Farm website.

was built in 1851 by wealthy plantation owner Nathaniel Cheairs and his wife, Susan. The story is told that there was a tradition in the Cheairs family for the men to marry women named Sarah, so when Nathaniel told his father that he intended to ask Susan McKissak to marry him, his father offered to pay the young man $5,000 in gold not to. Susan McKissak's father, one of the richest men in the area, heard of this and in reply he offered Cheairs all the bricks and slave labor he needed to build his home.

In the end, Cheairs married Susan and received both the gifts from his father-in-law and the $5,000 from his father—not a bad way to start out in life.

Rippavilla was sold out of the family in the 1920s, and the new owner modernized many of the finishes and also connected what was once a detached smokehouse and kitchen to the main building. Guided tours of the mansion last about 45 minutes and guests may also walk around the property, which includes an 1870s Freedman's School that was moved from another part of the county when it was threatened to be destroyed.

◖ Tennessee Museum of Early Farm Life

For an educational trip back in time, stop at the Tennessee Museum of Early Farm Life (5700 Main St., aka Hwy. 31, 931/381-3686, Fri.–Sat. 9 A.M.–3:30 P.M., adults $3, children and seniors $2), which displays farm, kitchen, and other useful implements used at Tennessee farms and homes in days gone by. Operated by a group of enthusiastic and knowledgeable retired farmers, the museum lovingly preserves plows, cultivators, seeders, wagons, and many other pieces of machinery that helped make a hard life just a bit easier for farmers and their families. You can see machinery and equipment used to make brooms, to make molasses, to sow seeds, to bale hay, and to cure pork. Through the descriptions provided by your tour guide, you begin to understand the ingenuity and inventiveness of these pioneers, as well as the hard work that went into fulfilling their basic needs.

OUTSIDE NASHVILLE

PHOTO COURTESY THE TENNESSEE DEPARTMENT OF TOURIST DEVELOPMENT

Cattle graze along the Natchez Trace Parkway.

AMISH COUNTRY

In 1944, three Amish families moved to Lawrence County. According to some accounts, they came seeking a place where they would not be required to send their children to large, consolidated secondary schools. They also were in search of land where they could farm and make a home.

Over the years the Amish population in Lawrence County has waxed and waned, and estimates put it between 100 and 200 families now. The Amish are known for their conservative dress, rejection of modern technology, including electricity, and their preference to keep to themselves. They are also excellent farmers, craftsmen, and cooks, devout Christians, and peace-lovers. Most of the Amish in this part of Tennessee speak English and Pennsylvania Dutch, and some also know German.

The Amish of Lawrence County live around the tiny town of Ethridge, a few miles north of Lawrenceburg. As you drive through the back roads that criss-cross the Amish area, you will be able to identify the Amish homes because they are old-fashioned farmhouses, without electricity wires, cars, or mechanized farm equipment. You will also notice their fields of corn, peanuts, wheat, oats, tobacco, hay, and oats, and you may see a black horse-drawn buggy – their primary form of transportation.

Many Amish sell goods, ranging from handmade furniture to molasses. As you drive, you will see signs advertising various products for sale. You are welcome to stop by and buy something. Remember that due to their religious beliefs, the Amish do not allow their pictures to be taken. Please respect this fact when you visit them.

If you prefer, you can explore Amish country with a guide on a wagon tour. Such tours are offered by local Lawrence County residents, who are not Amish. Each tour lasts about 90 minutes and will take you to several farms where you can meet the Amish and buy products from them. Tours are provided twice daily Monday–Saturday at 10 A.M. and 3:30 P.M. by the **Amish Country Store** (4011 Hwy. 43 N., 931/829-1621). The rate is $10 for adults. You can also call **Jerry's Amish Buggy and Wagon Tours** (931/629-5055).

If you want to drive through on your own, start in Ethridge and explore the narrow back roads bounded by Highway 43 on the east, State Route 242 on the west, Highway 20 on the north, and U.S. Route 64 on the south. You can pick up a free detailed map of Amish country, with specific farms identified, from the **Lawrence Chamber of Commerce** (1609 Locust Ave., aka Hwy 43, 931/762-4911, www.chamberofcommerce.lawrence.tn.us). You can also buy a map from the **Amish Country Mall** (4011 Hwy 43 N., 931/829-1621) for $3.

A half-dozen stores along Highway 43 just north of Ethridge sell Amish-made goods for those who don't have time to venture into Amish territory themselves. One of the best is **Dutch Country Bakery** (3939 Hwy. 43 N., 931/829-2147, Mon.-Sat. 7 A.M.-5 P.M.), which sells Amish baked goods, cheeses, and bulk goods. It also serves breakfast and lunch daily.

The Amish work Monday through Saturday. Sunday is their Sabbath, the day that they worship and spend time with family. You won't find any Amish farm stands or homes open for business on Sunday.

The museum is open on Friday and Saturday only, but call ahead for an appointment if you'd like to visit on a different day. It is located a few hundred yards behind the Rippavilla Plantation and was once called the Mule Museum, the name that is still reflected on the road sign at Rippavilla.

General Motors Plant
Spring Hill's Saturn automobile plant was re-tooled in 2007 to produce the Chevy Traverse cross-over vehicle. During the retooling and initial phases of production, the plant was closed for tours. To find out the current schedule call the General Motors Spring Hill Tour Office (Hwy. 31, 931/486-3869).

Accommodations
There is a **Best Western** (102 Kedron Pkwy., 931/486-1234, $90–130) in town with an outdoor pool, laundry facility, free full breakfast, fitness room, and business services.

COLUMBIA
Columbia is the seat of Maury County. Founded in 1809 and named for Christopher Columbus, Columbia was the commercial hub for Middle Tennessee's rich plantations. In 1850 it became the third-largest city in Tennessee, behind Nashville and Memphis. A decade later Maury County was the wealthiest county in the whole state. The city's prominence did not survive, however. The economic trauma of the Civil War was largely to blame.

◖ Ancestral Home of James Knox Polk
The United States' eleventh president, James Knox Polk, was born in North Carolina but moved to Middle Tennessee with his family when he was 11 years old. Before moving to town, Polk's family lived for several years on a farm north of Columbia, from where Polk's father ran successful plantations, speculated in land, and was involved in local politics.

The home where James Polk lived as a teenager and young man in Columbia is the only house remaining, besides the White House,

© SUSANNA HENIGHAN POTTER

OUTSIDE NASHVILLE

President James K. Polk's family home in Columbia is now a museum.

where Polk ever lived. It is now the Ancestral Home of James Knox Polk (301–305 W. 7th St., 931/388-2354, www.jameskpolk.com, April–Oct. Mon.–Sat. 9 A.M.–5 P.M., Sun. 1–5 P.M., Nov.–Mar. Mon.–Sat. 9 A.M.–4 P.M., Sun. 1–5 P.M., adults $7, seniors $6, youths 6–18 $5, children under 6 free), and home to a museum about Polk's life and presidency.

The home has a number of furnishings that belonged to President Polk and his wife, Sarah, while they lived at the White House. Other pieces come from Polk Place, the home that the couple planned and built in Nashville following the end of Polk's presidency in 1849. Sadly, Polk died of cholera just five months after leaving office and so had little opportunity to enjoy the home; Sarah Polk lived for another 42 years following her husband's death and she spent them all at Polk Place.

The Polk Home in Columbia was comfortable, but not luxurious, for its time. It was while living here that Polk began his career as a Tennessee lawyer, and eventually won his first seat in the U.S. House of

FIRST MONDAY

Until the widespread mechanization of farming, work animals were indispensable to Tennessee farmers. In many cases, mules were a farmer's most valuable asset – a good pair of mules could make a poor farmer rich.

Mules are a mix of jackass studs and mare horses. They can be either male or female, but most mules are sterile and cannot reproduce.

Mules were more expensive than horses or oxen, and more highly prized. They were said to be stronger, smarter, and more surefooted than other work animals. Their temperament can be stubborn, but some mules are easy and willing to work. For this reason, mule breeders were important, influential, and, often, quite wealthy.

No city in all of Tennessee is more closely associated with mules than Columbia. On the first Monday of April every year, the mule market opened and people flocked to Columbia to buy and sell mules. Other towns, including Lynchburg and Paris, were known for large "First Monday" sales, but Columbia's was the largest.

By 1900, word had spread as far as England about Columbia's First Monday. In that year, the British army sent buyers to Columbia. They bought every available mule and shipped them across the Atlantic to South Africa to aid their army fighting against the Boers.

As farmers adopted tractors and other mechanical farm equipment, mules lost their prominence. In the 1930s, Columbia

PHOTO COURTESY THE TENNESSEE DEPARTMENT OF TOURIST DEVELOPMENT

Mule Day in Columbia

resurrected First Monday and called it Mule Day, but it was foremost a festival, not a functional mule market. After a period of declining interest, the tradition of Mule Day returned in 1974 and has been going strong ever since.

Representatives. He would go on to serve 14 years in the House, four of them as Speaker. He was governor of Tennessee from 1839 to 1841 and defeated Henry Clay, a Whig, to become president in 1845. Polk's presidency was defined by his drive to expand the Union westward, and it was during his term in office that the United States added California, Texas, and Oregon to the territory of the United States.

The Polk Home provides a good introduction to this little-known, but nonetheless important, U.S. president.

Events

Columbia's **Mule Day** (931/381-9557, www.muleday.com) takes place over four days in mid-April. It includes mule sales, mule and donkey seminars, and mule shows and competitions. The highlight is the Mule Day Parade on Saturday morning, when thousands of people crowd to see school bands, mules, and colorful troops parade down the road. There is also live music, storytelling, dancing, gospel singing, and the crowning of the Mule Day Queen. Activities take place at various locations in Columbia, but the heart of Mule Day is the Maury County Park on Lion Parkway.

Accommodations

Columbia has more choices of chain hotels than any other city in Maury County. **Jameson Inn** (715 S. James M. Campbell Blvd., 931/388-3326, $85–90) is a 55-room hotel with all the amenities: complimentary breakfast, fitness center, free wireless Internet, pool, big televisions, movie channels, and ironing boards. Premium rooms add microwaves, refrigerators, and coffee-makers. The inn is located across the street from the Columbia Mall and downtown.

Locally owned, the **Richland Inn** (2405 Hwy. 31, 931/381-4500, www.columbiarichlandinn.com, $70–100) is a 147-room inn with singles, doubles, and suites. There is a continental breakfast and a family restaurant next door.

A host of motels are found around exit 46 on I-65, about 10 miles east of Columbia. They include **Comfort Inn** (1544 Bear Creek Pike, 931/388-2500, $75–100) and **Holiday Inn Express** (1558 Bear Creek Pike, 931/380-1227, $75–120).

For something special, sleep in the Carriage House at ⬛ **Rattle and Snap Plantation** (1522 N. Main St., aka Hwy. 243, Mount Pleasant, 931/379-1700, www.rattleandsnapplantation.com, $250), and you will enjoy your own private tour of one of the state's most famous antebellum homes. The Carriage House is a three-bedroom guesthouse located at the rear of the mansion. It includes two queen-sized bedrooms and a sleeping loft with two twin beds. There is also a kitchen, a sitting room, and a patio where guests can relax and prepare meals. No children are allowed, and smoking is not permitted. There is a two-night minimum stay.

Food

Located on the courthouse square, **Square Market and Cafe** (35 Public Sq., 931/840-3636, Mon.–Thurs. 9 A.M.–2:30 P.M., Fri. 9 A.M.–9 P.M., Sat. 10:30 A.M.–9 P.M., $6–19), serves breakfast and lunch throughout the week, and dinner on Friday and Saturday nights. The weekday menu features salads, sandwiches, and soups. The signature Polk's Roasted Pear Salad of greens, blue cheese, walnuts, and roasted-pear vinaigrette is a favorite for lunch. Heartier appetites can choose hot steamed sandwiches, or the Tennessee Hot Brown, a hot open-faced turkey sandwich topped with white sauce, cheddar cheese, and bacon. The café brews good coffee and the desserts are homemade. Weekend dinner includes entrées like baked salmon with dill caper sauce, spinach-and-garlic ravioli, and Eastern Shore crab cakes. There is live music too.

For country cooking, hearty breakfasts, and plate-lunch specials, head to **Bucky's Family Restaurant** (1102 Carmack Blvd., 931/381-2834, daily 5 A.M.–2 P.M., $4–12).

The best steakhouse in the area, **The Ole Lamplighter Inn** (1000 Riverside Dr., 931/381-3837, Mon.–Sat. 4:30–9 P.M., $10–26) will satisfy the biggest appetite with charbroiled steak, all-you-can-eat soup and salad buffet, bottomless soft drinks, plus seafood and shrimp options. The Lamplighter looks a bit like a log cabin from the outside, and inside it has a low-light tavern feel that hastens relaxation. Come here to enjoy good food at good prices.

Information

The **Middle Tennessee Visitors Bureau** (302 W. 7th St., 931/381-7176 or 888/852-1860, www.antebellum.com) operates a visitors center across the street from the James K. Polk house. The visitors center (931/840-8324) is open Monday–Saturday 9 A.M.–4 P.M.

OUTSIDE NASHVILLE

Land Between the Lakes

The narrow finger of land that lies between the Cumberland and Tennessee Rivers northeast of Clarkesville is a natural wonderland. Comprising 170,000 acres of land and wrapped by 300 miles of undeveloped river shoreline, the Land Between the Lakes National Recreation Area provides unrivaled opportunities to camp, hike, boat, or just simply drive through quiet wilderness. It is the third most-visited park in Tennessee, behind only the Smoky Mountains and Cherokee National Forest.

The area lies between what is now called Kentucky Lake (the Tennessee River) and Lake Barkley (the Cumberland River). At its narrowest point, the distance between these two bodies of water is only one mile. The drive from north to south is 43 miles. About one-third of the park is in Tennessee; the rest is in Kentucky. It is managed by the U.S. Forest Service, an agency of the U.S. Department of Agriculture.

SIGHTS
Driving south-to-north along the main road, or trace, that runs along the middle of the park, you will find the major attractions within Land Between the Lakes.

Great Western Iron Furnace
About 11 miles inside the park is the Great Western Iron Furnace, built by Brian, Newell, and Company in 1854. If you have traveled around this part of Tennessee much, you'll have come to recognize the distinctive shape of the old iron furnaces that dot the landscape in the counties between Nashville and the Tennessee River. Like the Great Western Furnace, these plants were used to create high-quality iron from iron ore deposits in the earth.

The Great Western Furnace operated for less than two years. By 1856 panic over reported slave uprisings and the coming of the Civil War caused the plant to shut down. It would never make iron again.

◖ The Homeplace
Just beyond the furnace is The Homeplace (270/924-2020, www.lbl.org, Mar.–Nov. daily 10 A.M.–5 P.M., $2–5), a living-history museum that re-creates an 1850 farmstead. At the middle of the 19th century, Between the Rivers was home to an iron ore industry and hundreds of farmers. These farmers raised crops and livestock for their own use, as well as to sell where they could. In 1850, about 10,000 people lived in Between the Rivers, including 2,500 slaves and 125 free blacks.

Staff dress up in period clothes and perform the labors that settlers would have done: They sow seeds in the spring, harvest in the summer and fall, and prepare the fields for the next year in the winter. The farm includes a dog trot cabin, where you can see how settlers would have lived, cooked, and slept. Out back there is a small garden, a plot of tobacco, pigs, sheep,

The Homeplace at Land Between the Lakes is a living history museum.

oxen, and barn. You may see farmers splitting shingles, working oxen, sewing quilts, making candles, or any other of the dozens of tasks that settlers performed on a regular basis.

The Homeplace publishes a schedule that announces when certain activities will take place, such as canning, shearing of sheep, or harvesting tobacco. Even if you come when there is no special program, you will be able to see staff taking on everyday tasks, and you can ask them about any facet of life on the frontier.

Elk and Bison Prairie

Archaeological evidence shows that elk and bison once grazed in Tennessee and Kentucky, including the area between the rivers. Settlers quickly destroyed these herds, however. Both bison and elk were easy to hunt, and they were desirable for their meat and skins. By 1800, bison had been killed off, and about 50 years later elk were gone too.

When Land Between the Lakes was created, elk and bison were reintroduced to the area. The **South Bison Range** across the road from the Homeplace is one of the places where bison now live. The bison herd that roams on about 160 acres here can sometimes be seen from the main road, or from side roads bordering the range.

You can see both bison and elk at the Elk and Bison Prairie, a 700-acre restoration project located near the mid-point of the Land Between the Lakes. In 1996, 39 bison were relocated from the south prairie here, and 29 elk were transported from Canada. Since then, the population of both animals has grown.

Visitors may drive through the range along a one-mile loop. Admission is $5 per vehicle. You are advised to take your time, roll down your windows, and keep your eyes peeled for a sign of the animals. The best time to view elk and bison is in the early morning or late afternoon. At other times of day, you will enjoy the sights and sounds of the grassland.

RECREATION

Promoting outdoor recreation is one of the objectives of Land Between the Lakes. Visitors can enjoy hiking, biking, or horseback riding;

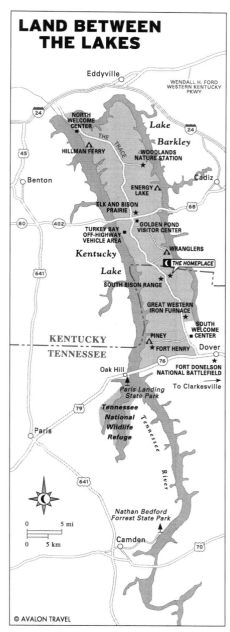

LAND BETWEEN THE LAKES

OUTSIDE NASHVILLE

hunting and fishing; and camping. There is even an area specially designated for all-terrain vehicles.

Trails

There are 200 miles of hiking trails in Land Between the Lakes. Some of these are also open for mountain biking and horseback riding.

The **Fort Henry Trails** are a network of 29.3 miles of trails near the southern entrance to the park, some of which follow the shoreline of the Kentucky Lake. The intricate network of trails allows hikers to choose from a three-mile loop to a much longer trek.

Access the trails from the South Welcome Station, or from the Fort Henry Hiking Trails parking area, at the end of Fort Henry Road. These trails criss-cross the grounds once occupied by the Confederate Fort Henry. They are for hikers only.

The **North-South Trail** treks the entire length of the Land Between the Lakes. From start to finish, it is 58.6 miles. Three backcountry camping shelters are available along the way for backpackers. The trail crosses the main road in several locations. Portions of the trail are open to horseback riders. The portion from the Golden Pond Visitor Center to the northern end is also open to mountain bikers.

A detailed map showing all hiking, biking, and horseback trails can be picked up at any of the park visitors centers. You can rent bikes at Hillman Ferry and Piney Campgrounds.

Fishing and Boating

Land Between the Lakes offers excellent fishing. The best season for fishing is spring, from April to June, when fish move to shallow waters to spawn. Crappie, largemouth bass, and a variety of sunfish may be caught at this time.

Summer and fall offer good fishing, while winter is fair. A fishing license from the state in which you will be fishing is required; these may be purchased from businesses outside of the park. Specific size requirements and open dates may be found at any of the visitors centers.

There are 19 different lake access points

where you can put in a boat. Canoe rentals are available at the Energy Lake Campground.

Hunting

Controlled hunting is one of the tools that the Forest Service uses to manage populations of wild animals in Land Between the Lakes. Hunting also draws thousands of visitors each year. The annual spring turkey hunt and fall deer hunts are the most popular.

Specific rules govern each hunt, and in many cases hunters must apply in advance for a permit. Hunters must also have a $20 LBL Hunter Use Permit, as well as the applicable state licenses. For details on hunting regulations, call the park at 270/924-2065.

CAMPING

There are nine campgrounds at Land Between the Lakes. All campgrounds have facilities for tent or trailer camping.

Most campgrounds are open from March 1 to November 1 annually. Tent campsites cost $12–13 per night; RV sites range $18–32, depending on whether it has electricity, water, and sewer services.

Reservations are accepted for select campsites at Piney, Energy Lake, Hillman's Ferry, and Wrangler Campgrounds. Reservations are available up to six months in advance; call the National Recreation Reservation Service at 877/444-6777 or go to www.recreation.gov.

Piney Campground

Located on the southern tip of Land Between the Lakes, **⟨ Piney Campground** is convenient to visitors arriving from the Tennessee side of the park. Piney has more than 300 campsites: 281 have electricity; 44 have electricity, water, and sewer; and 59 are primitive tent sites.

There are also nine rustic one-bedroom camping shelters with a ceiling fan, table and chairs, electric outlets, and large porch. Sleeping accommodations are one double bed and a bunk bed. Outside there is a picnic table and fire ring. There are no bathrooms; shelter guests use the same bathhouses as other campers. Camp shelters cost $35–37 per night and sleep up to four people.

Piney's amenities include a camp store, bike rental, archery range, playground, swimming beach, boat ramp, and fishing pier.

Energy Lake

Near the mid-point of Land Between the Lakes, **Energy Lake Campground** has tent and trailer campsites, electric sites, and group camp facilities.

Backcountry Camping

Backcountry camping is allowed year-round in Land Between the Lakes. All you need is a backcountry permit and the right gear to enjoy unlimited choices of campsites along the shoreline or in the woodlands.

PRACTICALITIES

There are no restaurants or hotels in Land Between the Lakes. Drive to Dover for food and accommodation other than camping.

The Forest Service maintains a useful website about Land Between the Lakes at www.lbl. org. You can also call 270/924-2000 to request maps and information sheets. The park headquarters is located at the Golden Pond Visitor Center across the Kentucky state line.

When you arrive, stop at the nearest welcome or visitors center for up-to-date advisories and activity schedules. Each of the welcome centers and the visitors center are open daily 9 A.M.–5 P.M.

The **Land Between the Lakes Association** (800/455-5897, www.friendsoflbl.org) organizes volunteer opportunities and publishes a detailed tour guide to the park, which includes historical and natural anecdotes.

FORT DONELSON NATIONAL BATTLEFIELD

On Valentine's Day in 1862, Union forces attacked the confederate Fort Donelson on the banks of the Cumberland River. Fort Donelson National Battlefield (Hwy. 79, 931/232-5706, www.nps.gov/fodo) is now a national park. A visitors center with an exhibit, gift shop,

and information boards is open daily 8 A.M.– 4:30 P.M. The 15-minute video does a good job of describing the battle and its importance in the Civil War.

A driving tour takes visitors to Fort Donelson, which overlooks the Cumberland River and may be one of the most picturesque forts in Tennessee. The fort is an earthenwork fort, built by Confederate soldiers and slaves over a period of about seven months.

You are also guided to the **Dover Hotel** (Petty St., 931/232-5706), which was used as the Confederate headquarters during the battle. The hotel, built between 1851 and 1853, is a handsome wood structure and has been restored to look as it did during the battle. It is located a few blocks away from downtown Dover. The hotel is open from noon to 4 P.M. on weekends from Memorial Day to Labor Day.

The **National Cemetery,** established after the war, was built on grounds where escaped slaves lived in a so-called "contraband camp" during the Civil War. The camp was established by the Union army to accommodate slaves who fled behind Union lines during the war. The freedmen and women worked for the Union army, often without pay. It was not until 1853 that the Union army allowed blacks to join as soldiers.

There are more than five miles of hiking trails at Fort Donelson National Battlefield, including the three-mile River Circle Trail and four-mile Donelson Trail. Both hikes begin at the visitors center. Picnic tables are located next to the river near the old fort.

DOVER

A small town set at the southern shore of the Cumberland River, Dover is a major gateway to the Land Between the Lakes. It is also the place where Gen. Ulysses S. Grant earned the nickname "Unconditional Surrender" during the Civil War.

Accommodations

Located right next to Fort Donelson National Cemetery, **(The Riverfront Plantation Inn** (165 Plantation Ln., 931/232-9492, www.riverfrontplantation.com, $85–110) is the best place

UNCONDITIONAL SURRENDER

The Union army won its first major victory of the Civil War at Fort Donelson in 1862. Following unexpected defeats at Manassas and Wilson's Creek in 1861, the Federal victory at Fort Donelson was cause for celebration for supporters of the Union.

The Union forces were attracted to Fort Donelson, and nearby Fort Henry, because of the area's strategic importance. In an age of steamships and river transportation, the Cumberland and Tennessee Rivers were superhighways into the heart of Dixie. Union reconnaissance found that the forts, built hurriedly by the Confederates to protect the rivers, were vulnerable.

Fort Henry fell to a force of Union gunboats on February 6, 1862. The boats bombarded the fort for more than an hour before the fort surrendered. Almost 2,500 Confederate soldiers escaped and fled to Fort Donelson, which had a stronger position.

Meanwhile, Union forces were marching over land to Fort Donelson. By February 13, some 15,000 Union troops had nearly encircled the fort, under the command of Brig. Gen. Ulysses S. Grant. But the Union strategy at Fort Donelson was not land-based alone. On the morning of Valentine's Day, a Union fleet of gunboats attacked Fort Donelson from the Cumberland River. They were not successful, however, due to the fort's protected position. After 90 minutes, the ships retreated.

Despite having repulsed the river attack, Confederate commanders were not optimistic. They knew that the Union army was receiving reinforcements every day and had virtually surrounded Fort Donelson. Confederates feared a siege. So the South's commanders, including Generals John Floyd, Gideon Pillow, and Simon Buckner, decided that their best option was to abandon Fort Donelson and retreat to Nashville, where they could regroup. But in order to retreat, the Confederates had

© SUSANNA HENIGHAN POTTER

Fort Donelson is peaceful now; on Valentine's Day, 1862, it was the site of furious fighting.

to push the Federals back far enough to clear a route of escape.

On February 15, the Confederates attacked, and they won important ground from the Federals. Unfortunately for the South, poor leadership and indecision led to a bad order to retreat, just when they had gained their new ground. Gen. Grant immediately launched a vigorous counter-attack and the Federals retook the ground they had just lost and gained even more.

Seeing the writing on the walls, Southern Generals Floyd and Pillow slipped away overnight, leaving Gen. Buckner, a former friend and schoolmate of Gen. Grant, in command. A few hundred men under the command of Nathan Bedford Forrest also escaped overnight rather than be taken prisoner. On the morning of February 16, Buckner wrote to Grant asking for the terms of surrender.

In Grant's famous reply, he said no terms other than "unconditional and immediate" surrender would be accepted. Buckner surrendered, and 13,000 Confederate men were taken prisoner. The path to the heart of the Confederacy was now open, and Grant earned a new nickname: "Unconditional Surrender" Grant.

to stay in Dover. A bed-and-breakfast inn with four rooms and a commanding view of the Cumberland River, this is truly a distinctive retreat. Originally built in 1859, the inn was mostly destroyed by fire in 1865. It served as a Union hospital during the Civil War. After the war, the house was rebuilt and remains much the same today.

The inn is a white brick building, graceful and stately above the river. Guest rooms are neat and cozy, and are named after Confederate generals, including Nathan Bedford Forrest and James Longstreet. All have views of the river, and two rooms may be rented together to form a two-bedroom suite. A hearty breakfast is served on the sunny dining porch overlooking the river.

Just west of the entrance to Land Between the Lakes, the **Dover Inn Motel** (1545 Donelson Pkwy., 931/232-5556, $60–70) has both traditional motel rooms and cabins with full kitchens. All rooms have telephones, cable TV, air-conditioning, and coffee makers. They cater to hunters and fishermen who are going to Land Between the Lakes but don't want to camp. There is a swimming pool on the property.

Food

The most elegant dining in Dover is at the **Plantation Inn Dining Room** (165 Plantation Ln., 931/232-9492, Thurs.–Sat. 5–9 P.M., Sun. 10 A.M.–2 P.M., $10–20). Located in a bed-and-breakfast overlooking the Cumberland River,

the Plantation Inn serves upscale dinners in its old-fashioned dining room or on the breezy dining porch. Country Cordon Bleu, crab cakes, and cheesy vegetarian pasta are a few of the options on the dinner menu. Entrées are served with your choice of a half-dozen different side dishes, including truffle mashed potatoes and squash casserole. Reservations are recommended, but not essential.

For something entirely different, head to the **B&M Dairy Freeze** (610 Donelson Pkwy., 931/232-5927, daily 10:30 A.M.–7 P.M., $4–8), a casual restaurant with burgers, hot dogs, and ice cream located just west of downtown Dover.

Located downtown, **The Dover Grille** (310 Donelson Pkwy., 931/232-7919, daily 7 A.M.–9 P.M., $5–12) serves burgers, dinner plates, southwestern platters, pasta, and salads.

Several miles east of the town is the **Log Cabin Cafe** (1394 Hwy. 79, 931/232-0220, Mon.–Sat. 6 A.M.–9 P.M., Sun. 6 A.M.–3 P.M., $6–15). The café serves traditional southern food in a log cabin. It is a popular pit stop for workmen; their breakfast will fuel you all day long.

Information

The **Stewart County Chamber of Commerce** (1008 Moore Rd., 931/232-8290, www.stewartcountyvacation.com) provides visitor information.

OUTSIDE NASHVILLE

MOON NASHVILLE
Avalon Travel
A member of the Perseus Books Group
1700 Fourth Street
Berkeley, CA 94710, USA
www.moon.com

Editor and Series Manager: Kathryn Ettinger
Copy Editor: Amy Scott
Graphics Coordinator: Sean Bellows
Production Coordinator: Sean Bellows
Cover Designer: Sean Bellows
Map Editor: Albert Angulo
Cartographers: Chris Markiewicz, Kat Bennett, and
  Brice Ticen

ISBN-13: 978-1-59880-404-1

Some photos and illustrations are used by permission and are the property of the original copyright owners.

Front cover photo: Guitar © Elena Elisseeva/123rf.com
Title page photo: Grand Ole Opry sign, Courtesy of Tennessee Department of Tourist Development

Printed in the United States

ABOUT THE AUTHOR

Susanna Henighan Potter

Susanna Henighan Potter was born and raised in the foothills of the Smoky Mountains in east Tennessee. Chilhowee Mountain stood sentry over the old farmhouse where she grew up, imagining trips to faraway times and places. Despite her best efforts, however, Susanna's upbringing was well grounded in Tennessee things: the wail of old-time bluegrass music, the bright orange of the Tennessee Volunteers, and the electricity of Friday-night high school football. Family outings were almost always journeys to one or another of Tennessee's natural attractions, and she became a seasoned car camper.

Susanna graduated from Oberlin College with a degree in economics and enough clips from the *Oberlin Review* to land a job as a reporter in the British Virgin Islands. For several years, she wrote for local newspapers and filed reports for the Associated Press, returning to Tennessee for regular visits. In 2006, her first Moon Handbook, *Moon Virgin Islands*, was published.

Writing *Moon Nashville* has been a journey of rediscovery for Susanna. It meant taking a second look at many places that were part of the landscape of her childhood. It also meant taking that thrilling first look at some parts of the state that were delightfully new to her.

Susanna lives with her husband in the Virgin Islands, where she works for the Government of the British Virgin Islands. She returns to Tennessee to visit her family several times a year.